COUИTER
CULTUЯE

ANSWERING A WOKE
CULTURE WITH LOVE,
LIGHT, AND LIFE

COUNTER
CULTURE

DUANE SHERIFF

CONTENTS

FOREWORD

I was so honored when Pastor Duane Sherriff asked me to write the foreword to his new book, *Counterculture—Answering a Woke Culture with Love, Light, and Life.* I am blessed to call him my friend and fellow pastor. He is a watchman on the wall sounding the alarm to the dangers of the "woke culture" threatening our freedom and liberties in America.

I believe the Lord has placed Pastor Duane on the front lines of this culture war we in America are facing. I am most thankful that he is responding properly, which is with the love, the light, and the life of God revealed in scripture.

In this book, Pastor Duane has gone to the root of the issue and identified the fact that we must establish a counterculture of grace and truth to combat this evil that has even made its way into the pulpits of American churches.

I read an article recently that said "wokeism" (as it is being called) is now a "new religion" moving like a tidal wave through every facet of Western culture, shaping and redefining society. It masquerades under the guise of compassion and justice, but underneath, it is an evil ideology. The only answer for this evil is the gospel of the Lord Jesus Christ.

Patrick Henry said, "The great pillars of all government and of social life are virtue, morality, and religion. This is the armor... and this alone, that renders us invincible." If we will turn the tide of evil making its way into our society, we must have God's help, which comes through His Word.

You will quickly observe that Pastor Duane is no hireling; he is a true shepherd of the flock of God who doesn't run when he sees the wolf coming. The best way I can describe his ministry style is to say that it's full of grace, and yet, there is absolutely no compromise of the truth.

I believe the book that you now hold in your hands is a desperately needed "now word" for the body of Christ. Thank you, Pastor Duane, for your obedience to write this book.

MARK COWART
Senior Pastor, Church For All Nations
Director of the Practical Government
School, Charis Bible College

CHAPTER 1

CULTURAL REVOLUTION

In the opening of *A Tale of Two Cities*, Charles Dickens describes the condition of France during the French Revolution: "It was the best of times, it was the worst of times; it was the age of wisdom, it was the age of foolishness; it was the epoch of belief, it was the epoch of incredulity; it was the season of light, it was the season of darkness." I firmly believe that this short prelude to a historical fiction novel could have been written about the United States of America today.

Whether we know it or not, we are experiencing a cultural revolution. Because it is not a bloody one, most are completely unaware of the consequences of these radical times. Never in our country's history has there been such an abuse of political power as we are witnessing today. City mayors, state governors, and other high-ranking politicians

3

are attempting to destroy small businesses and livelihoods under the guise of protecting public health from COVID-19. Churches are being shut down, yet liquor stores and cannabis shops remain open. Politicians are free to move about while we are under strict quarantine. Many are coming to a newfound faith in Jesus, yet others are renouncing their Christianity. The great awakening to God's righteousness by faith is met with self-righteousness and virtue signaling that has the potential to destroy the hearts and minds of an entire generation.

However, to quote Dickens, these "worst of times" are also the "best of times." While the devil is counterfeiting the Great Awakening with the "woke" movement, God is working. Originally, the term "woke" simply meant being awake and not asleep regarding prejudice and injustice, or being alert to injustice in society, especially concerning racism. Today it has evolved into man's self-righteousness, which is the deepest form of pride.

Many pretend to care for others and have compassion but are completely self-absorbed. It's all about how others perceive them rather than dealing with real injustices around them. It becomes, "Look at me, I'm aware" and "I care, so that makes me a better person." "Wokeness" is more virtuous than actually fixing the injustices that they claim to be awakened to.

God is waking people up to sin, and repentance is changing their hearts, causing them to treat one another with God's love and justice for one another. For every evil work of the enemy, God is blessing and prospering His people. A great light is burgeoning on the horizon, countering the gross darkness of this culture. Darkness is being exposed and expelled. In a culture of hate, death, and darkness, we as the church need to be the counterculture of love, life, and light. Lockdowns, political correctness, censorship, and cancel culture must be met with freedom of movement, thought, and speech. "Critical Race Theory" must be met with "Critical *Grace* Theory."

Critical Race Theory is a movement based on a hate for America, its founders, and the Constitution's ideology. It claims the country is hopelessly flawed and ripe with systemic racism. It suggests that the Constitution is a racist document, and all white people are racist—even if they don't know it. Their solution is to tear it all down and rebuild it into some other image that is never made clear, at least in all the research I have done. Everything, and I mean everything, is about race.

Those who are a part of the counterculture know and believe that the answer and solution to all our sin and problems is grace. Make no mistake, even now Jesus is building His church, and the gates of hell will not prevail against it (see Matt. 16:18).

SUBCULTURE

I have always known that culture has a role to play in social evolution, but there were many aspects of it that were a mystery to me. How does culture affect local churches? What role does it play in the Kingdom of God? Do we create culture, or does it create us? Once created, does it change us, or do we change the culture? Is it by design or default? What role does it play in God's plan for His church, if any? While I will get into detail concerning culture in the next chapter, I wanted to give some background beforehand.

The more research that I've done for this book, the more I have discovered that the church at large has become a sub-culture to a world's culture gone awry.

A subculture shares common traits with the dominant culture. Differences can coexist because of underlying, similar values and common goals. A subculture runs parallel with a dominant culture to fit in. However, Christ never intended us to be a subculture—to "go along to get along." We are called to cultivate a counterculture—His counterculture, a Kingdom of God's culture.

A counterculture runs in opposition to the dominant culture. A counterculture can influence and change the dominant culture for good—or bad. Just like the world, the Kingdom of God has a culture. Instead of sharing common traits with the world, the Kingdom's culture runs in complete opposition to it.

In the King James Version of the Bible, Matthew 11:12 says that *"The kingdom of heaven suffereth violence, and the violent take it by force."* The same chapter and verse in the New Living Translation says: *"the Kingdom of Heaven has been forcefully advancing, and violent people are attacking it."* This verse points out that the world's culture is not friendly to God's truth and righteousness. One glance into society today reveals that every good, moral, and decent principle that originates in God's Kingdom is under assault.

There are not just differences of opinion on good and evil. Instead, there is a hatred for and attempt to eliminate anything God calls good. Romans 1:30 declares people will be not just disobedient to Him, but *"haters of God, violent, proud, boasters, inventors of evil things."* This path leads to a reprobate or depraved mind; one void of the knowledge of God (see Rom. 1:28).

Paul warns a young pastor, Timothy, that in the last days perilous times will come:

> *People will be lovers of themselves, lovers of money, boastful, proud, abusive, disobedient to their parents, ungrateful, unholy, without love, unforgiving, slanderous, without self-control, brutal, not lovers of the good, treacherous, rash, conceited, lovers of pleasure rather than lovers of God—having a form of godliness but denying its power. Have nothing to do with such people.*
>
> 2 TIMOTHY 3:2-5 (NIV)

The "woke" movement has a form of godliness but denies the power of the cross. We are to avoid this philosophy and turn from it unto the grace of our Lord Jesus Christ.

GOD'S COUNTERCULTURE

"These who have turned the world upside down have come here too" (Acts 17:6). The apostles were not considered as men who "went along to get along." They were not afraid to be politically incorrect. They refused to allow politics or politicians to dictate their way of life, speech, or thought. In fact, in the face of Caesar, the emperor of the most powerful empire at that time, they declared that Jesus is King and Lord of all. They were firmly rooted in the fact that they were to

affect the world's dominant culture and not allow the world to influence them or their work for the Kingdom of God.

Are we turning the world upside down, or is the church allowing itself to be silenced with political correctness, government abuses of power, the corrupt national press, and other institutions? Our nation was founded on Judeo-Christian values, religious freedom, and a representative republic. In that founding, the church affected the culture in a positive, progressive way. In the United States of America, we have enjoyed the power and freedoms invested in "We the People" for more than 240 years. However, for the past 50-plus years that has changed.

The dominant culture has been determined to remove God from all arenas of public expression and has succeeded—from attempting to destroy our Constitution to disrespect for the flag; from hatred of the founders to the rewriting of history; from the defunding and dismantling of police forces to the looting and burning down of major cities. The very core of our republic's foundation is under violent assault.

The dark seeds of Socialism and Marxism are taking root as many of our major cities are experiencing complete lockdowns destroying people's livelihoods and careers. Churches are threatened and called super-spreaders of the COVID-19 virus. Pastors have been arrested for obeying God in keeping their church doors open (see Heb. 10:25).

Likewise, worshipers have been fined and threatened in following God's Word (to fear God, not people). Prayer, Bibles, and the Ten Commandments were removed from our schools long ago, and now some California school districts are eliminating Christmas, Thanksgiving, and Easter from their school calendar.

AT WAR WITH EVIL

We are at war with evil forces, principalities, and powers at work in our culture (see Eph. 6:10-12). These evil forces poison the hearts of individuals and are destroying the soul of a nation. The United States of America is collapsing under demonic assault, and many believers are passive in their opposition to this encroachment and prefer to be a subculture allowing God to be taken out of the fabric of civil society. We have allowed moral absolutes to be replaced by moral relativity and evolving truth. History has proven that once you remove God and moral absolutes from any society, death, destruction, and human suffering aren't far behind.

John Adams (one of America's founders and our second President) wrote: "Our constitution was made only for a moral and religious people. It is wholly inadequate to the government of any other." The glue that holds our government and society together is anchored in these moral absolutes:

- God's righteousness: Righteousness according to God, not man without God. Righteousness rooted in Scripture, not philosophy or self-righteousness.

- Love: Love for God, family, each other, and country. Love that is God's character and nature as defined in 1 Corinthians 13:4-8. Love that never changes versus the ever-changing ways of mankind.

- Basic decency toward our fellow man: The golden rule, "Do unto others as you would have them do unto you." Valuing God's image in all people and treating one another with respect.

- Justice: God's justice for all. Justice that is unbiased, without prejudice, and meted out with righteousness and mercy.

- Mercy: Grace is when we get what we don't deserve. Mercy is when we don't get what we deserve: *"Blessed are the merciful, for they will be shown mercy"* (Matt. 5:7 NIV).

- Forgiveness: Forgiveness releases others of debt or the "you owe me" mentality. God has released us of a great debt of sin that we could not pay. He has forgiven us our trespasses and calls us to forgive one another.

- Reconciliation: The entire Bible testifies of God reconciling us back unto Him in Jesus Christ. We are separated from God by sin and could not bridge the gap. Jesus died to bridge that gap in paying the price for our sin and bringing us back to God through the cross. Now that we are reconciled to God in Christ, we are to be reconciled with one another.

These are just a few of the absolutes God has called us to in Christ Jesus.

The negative culture we see today is, in part, the church's fault. I'm not saying this to condemn anyone but rather to wake us up. We are called to speak out and stand up in loving opposition to a dominant culture of hate, death, and darkness. In both word and deed, we are to be a culture of love, life, and light.

FREEDOM WITHIN BOUNDARIES

As the counterculture, the church is the only hope to break the powers of darkness in our world. We get to be a part of the Great Awakening that is coming and is here now. The saving power of Jesus is the only thing that can transform the culture or change politics and have a profound effect on our nation. Politics is downstream from culture. As the gospel affects people's hearts, it will affect culture, thereby changing our politics. Today's politics simply reflect a corrupt culture. We can only save our nation, change the culture, and affect politics one heart at a time, one good deed at a time, one vote at a time. Cultural reforms are only possible when there is revival in our hearts.

CULTURAL REFORMS ARE ONLY POSSIBLE WHEN THERE IS REVIVAL IN OUR HEARTS.

In its purest form, politics involves our shared set of beliefs regarding justice and civil discourse as well as our social order. Politics should be an agreed set of boundaries within our shared political community. As a people who are self-governed, there should be certain kinds of behavior expected of everyone who wants to live in a civilized society. While there is to be freedom to disagree over many things in co-existing as a people and nation, there should be agreement concerning boundaries no matter what the political party. Public order, civil discourse, transparency, and truth within government and the press are essential to our survival as a Republic. Fair and honest elections are vital to all people in a shared community of freedom.

We must see a revival within our social community and shared institutions such as public schools, colleges, media, political parties, etc., or we will collapse under the weight of all the corruption we see today. Good government is how we coexist within the divergence of opinions and behaviors we see in our world today. The "Great Awakening" will influence the culture and have a positive effect on our politics, leading to policies that make for a just and righteous society.

> And it shall come to pass in the last days, says God, that I will pour out of My Spirit on all flesh; your sons and your daughters shall prophesy, your young men shall see visions, your old men shall dream dreams.
>
> ACTS 2:17

God's Spirit is being poured out on us to make a mega-positive difference for God on earth. "It's the best of times"—and the best is yet to come for us, the church, as we continue to become a counterculture.

CHAPTER 2

WHAT IS CULTURE?

According to one definition, culture is "the behavior and beliefs characteristic of a particular social, ethnic, or age group." Different churches have their own unique cultures or atmosphere. You can visit a church and feel the culture even if you can't explain it. The atmosphere of belief systems and group-think is as real as a thick fog on an October morning as the sun begins to rise in the woods.

When you walk into a new church building, most of the time you get an immediate sense of "I'm welcome here" or "Where is the nearest exit?" Each kind of culture has its own way of functioning. Culture, especially church culture, develops over time. It can be positive or negative.

Chick-fil-A has mastered a warm, serving culture. Regardless of your request, it will be met with a friendly, "My pleasure." They don't have a copyright on this, though it is a great business model.

In my early Christian experience, I encountered many negative cultures in church. When I was younger, the cultures of most churches I attended were condemning, judgmental, and convinced me that God was displeased with me. Repeated exposure to those churches' belief systems led to a sense of failure and insecurity as a believer.

The moment I realized that I was called to be a pastor, the memory of what I experienced in my youth concerned me and I realized that I unconsciously developed a belief that all churches were bad (how sad). Once I discovered that I could create culture by design rather than be a victim by default, I said yes to being a pastor and determined to create a church culture of forgiveness, grace, and righteousness by faith. I wanted us to demonstrate that not only does God love us, but He even likes us! This was important in producing a sense of security and victory in this life.

Within any culture are certain pillars that uphold and support the values of the people. These values (or lack thereof), shared understanding, and common language are held by all who are identified within that group. In its purest form, culture is living out what we believe. However, culture is not just "what we believe" but "how we behave." For example, we can believe family is a priority, but if we aren't making time for our family, the culture of our home won't reflect what we say we believe.

As a pastor, I understand that culture begins with me and the leadership of the church. Whatever culture we establish, the people will follow. When building our church, I knew that I wanted the dominant leadership culture to be one of honor, unity, and trust. I also knew that it had to start within our leadership team.

Very early in our church's history, we committed to these three principles:

1. Honor each other's gifts, anointing, and wisdom.
2. Maintain the Unity of the Spirit in the bond of peace.
3. Trust in one another.

It is known in our church culture as the HUT principle. It wasn't enough to just say we believed in these three things; it had to be how we behaved in our relationships with each other. Once I saw that our team operated in these principles, we set out to develop a culture of loving God and people while serving both within the church body. Our goal was to make our culture of "love and servanthood" apparent to anyone who walked through our doors.

SALT, LIGHT, AND A CITY ON A HILL

In the world today, hate, death, and darkness are dominating the cultural landscape. These three forces have become the norm rather than the exception. We face the challenge of raising our children and grandchildren in a culture of corruption and destruction. While this darkness works to harden the hearts and minds of a generation, God has called us (the church) to be a counterculture of love, life, and light.

> *You are the salt of the earth. But what good is salt if it has lost its flavor? Can you make it salty again? It will be thrown out and trampled underfoot as worthless. You are the light of the world—like a city on a hilltop that cannot be hidden. No one lights a lamp and then puts it under a basket. Instead, a lamp is placed on a stand, where it gives light to everyone in the house. In the same way, let your good deeds shine out for all to see, so that everyone will praise your heavenly Father.*
>
> MATTHEW 5:13-16 (NLT)

Notice that we are *not* called the salt of the church. Instead, Jesus identifies us as the "salt of the earth." Based on the need, salt does three things: 1) preserves, 2) destroys bacteria, and 3) adds flavor to food. Before the invention of refrigeration, meat was preserved with salt. The same salt that preserved the meat destroyed any bacteria from spoiling it, all while adding to its flavor. Likewise, we are commissioned on earth to preserve all things near and dear to the heart of God while destroying the works of Satan. We preserve people while destroying the powers of darkness. Just like salt, if we lose our flavor or influence, we are worthless or useless in countering the world's destructive culture. Also notice that we are called "light of the world" and a "city set on a hill."

Light, by nature, exposes and expels darkness. We cannot hide ourselves away; rather, we need to let our light—good works—shine before everyone to glorify our Father in heaven. We cannot be ashamed of God's Word—the Bible—and its power to change hearts, minds, and lives. We must be both (salt and light) by our new nature in Christ. This is who we are and should now affect all we do and how we behave.

As a "city on a hill" we are not to hide behind four walls. Our self-imposed quarantine must be broken, allowing us to share the gospel that is the power of God for salvation to everyone who believes (see Rom. 1:16). As the people of God, we cannot be hidden—we need to let our lights shine so that when people see our good works, they will see the glory of God. What a powerful promise and truth. Our light (good works) is not before God (self-righteousness) but rather before people. Our good works do not impress God, but they do bless the people. Jesus is our righteousness before God, and our good works are before men and women. We must become "super-spreaders" of the gospel.

For decades, the church has allowed the world to cause us to live under house arrest. Because of this, the world is collapsing due to the weight of sin and the absence of light. Instead of the principles of God, the philosophies of men dominate the public discourse leading to the destruction of people's lives. Paul addresses these issues in Colossians 2:6-8:

> *As you therefore have received Christ Jesus the Lord, so walk in Him, rooted and built up in Him and established in the faith, as you have been taught, abounding in it with thanksgiving. Beware lest anyone cheat you through philosophy and empty deceit, according to the tradition of men, according*

to the basic principles of the world, and not according to Christ.

Those of us who are followers of Christ must now be established in our faith, abounding with thanksgiving. It is imperative that God's Kingdom principles be taught. Unfortunately, most people have not been taught what God's Word says about the cultural issues we face today. Worse yet, many are being taught the philosophies of this world that can cause their faith in Jesus and His Word to plummet or become nonexistent.

My people are destroyed for lack of knowledge. Because you have rejected knowledge, I also will reject you from being priest for Me; because you have forgotten the law of your God, I also will forget your children.

HOSEA 4:6

Christians are being destroyed for a lack of knowledge of God's Word. Sadly, many are now suffering from this ignorance of truth. We must repent and receive God's Word for our sakes and future generations. Psalm 107:20 says, "*He sent His word and healed them, and delivered them from their* destructions." This next great awakening will usher in a hunger for revelation of God's Word, the Bible.

As you know, to spoil is to go from good to bad. If we are spoiled, we no longer have a positive effect in and on our world. Our influence as a "city on a hill" and our impact as "salt and light" is diminished. These scriptures reveal there are four things that spoil us as Christians: 1) human philosophies, 2) empty (or enemy) deceit, 3) traditions, and 4) basic worldly principles. Let's look at each on in more detail.

1. HUMAN PHILOSOPHIES

A philosophy is simply a way of thinking. It is not bad in and of itself. God has a philosophy about things as well, but when human philosophies are exalted above God's, it can spoil the mind of a believer. Today we are offered all kinds of solutions to our problems that contradict God's Word. *"There is a way that appears to be right, but in the end it leads to death"* (Prov. 14:12 NIV). Any secular worldview always ends in some type of death.

A secular worldview is a human philosophy, human opinion, and human way of thinking apart from God's influence. One damaging secular worldview is the so-called destruction of the planet known as "global warming," currently labeled "climate change" in response to the recent record cold snaps. "They" say we can save the planet and ourselves by giving up all our God-given freedoms and submitting to corrupt government mandates. "They" try to convince us that if we don't, we will all die in so many years—the number changes as the predictions are proven lies. This tactic of fear, worry, and anxiety could cause us to give up freedom.

In contrast, a biblical worldview is the complete opposite. God's philosophy says that He created the world, upholds it, and has preserved it for the day of judgment (see Heb. 11:3; 1:3; 2 Pet. 3:7). At His appearing and Kingdom, He will save us and the planet, creating a new heaven and a new earth, and nothing but righteousness will reign. There are enough opposing philosophies between the world and God to fill several books, but the point to be made here is that the world's philosophies will spoil you while God's philosophies will produce faith, hope, and peace.

2. EMPTY DECEIT

Our culture is collapsing under the weight of lies and distortions on a daily basis. Mainstream media is filled with deception and coordinated falsehoods. True journalism has been replaced by constant hit pieces launched on anyone who opposes their agenda. In today's world culture, truth has been replaced with bold-faced lies, and while we could blame the station owners and journalists, the Word says that ultimately Satan is the father of all lies:

> You are of your father the devil, and the desires of your father you want to do. He was a murderer from the beginning, and does not stand in the truth, because there is no truth in him. When he speaks a lie, he speaks from his own resources, for he is a liar and the father of it.
>
> JOHN 8:44

The book of Revelation in the Bible describes the kind of people who have allowed Satan's influence a place in their lives:

> But the cowardly, unbelieving, abominable, murderers, sexually immoral, sorcerers, idolaters, and all liars shall have their part in the lake which burns with fire and brimstone, which is the second death.
>
> REVELATION 21:8

Notice that the first word of this list is *cowardly*. The King James translation says "fearful," which in *Strong's Concordance* means "timid or to dread" (*deilos*, G1169). I know this may sound harsh, but remember, as people who are in Christ, fear should have no place in our lives. People being afraid to speak up are in the same camp as those who lie. God is calling us to repent from being afraid and from lying.

> *Have I not commanded you? Be strong and of good courage; do not be afraid, nor be dismayed, for the Lord your God is with you wherever you go.*
>
> JOSHUA 1:9

> *For God has not given us a spirit of fear, but of power and of love and of a sound mind.*
>
> 2 TIMOTHY 1:7

> *Fearing people is a dangerous trap, but trusting the Lord means safety.*
>
> PROVERBS 29:25 (NLT)

Our greatest success in ministry is not that we offend no one by withholding the truth, but rather that we please God by speaking the truth in love. Our fear to speak up or out is as egregious to God as the lies of our culture that are destroying the innocent and unlearned. While God hasn't called us to be rude or mean, He has commanded us to be bold and courageous. In John 5:44 Jesus states, *"How can you believe, who receive honor from one another, and do not seek the honor that comes from the only God?"*

No one wants to be rejected, but we must overcome any fear knowing God has accepted us. Luke 6:26 declares, *"Woe to you when all men speak well of you, for so did their fathers to the false prophets.*" The only way to have everyone speak well of you is to be a false prophet. Generationally, false prophets are the ones adored.

Despite these and many more promises regarding fear, people are afraid to speak out. The world watched as Judge Brett Kavanaugh's character was assassinated during his confirmation hearing to the Supreme Court. Not only were lies told about him, but people sought his and his family's destruction. Many were hesitant to speak out, in fear of similar attacks being launched at them personally. However, being censored, banned from social media, or outright attacked is just the beginning of what is to come if we remain silent.

We are to be a counterculture to vain deceit. How? By speaking the truth in love. Ephesians 4:15 declares that: "*speaking the truth in love, may grow up into him in all things, which is the head, even Christ*" (KJV). Speaking the truth in love facilitates growth and health. Lies ensnare and poison one's soul and the culture. Any speech today that is contrary to the lies and falsehoods of government elites or media propaganda is subject to censorship in many social platforms.

While we are never to be rude or mean-spirited (you'll be accused of those regardless), we should never fear being direct and honest. Our nation is imploding under the weight of lies and obsession for power. God is calling us to repent of being fearful and lying. The truth must be spoken in love or people will die in their sins and give an account to God.

3. TRADITIONS

Not all tradition is bad, but tradition that no longer serves its original purpose can be serious. Many vote out of tradition and have no idea what they are voting for. It's just the way we've done it for decades. I've always encouraged people to look at our two major political party platforms and see which one is the closest to God's Word and philosophy. In many cases it wouldn't matter because people are married to their traditions and not to Jesus and His Word.

Jesus taught that human traditions could make the Word of God of no effect (see Mark 7:13). When we exalt tradition, especially those rooted in lies, we cancel out God's Word in our lives. Many today are bound by generational lies and traditions that violate God's Word, others by generational poverty and the welfare state.

I was caught in generational poverty. It had become a way of life or tradition in my family for so long that we just accepted it. Poverty was considered who we were and how we were to behave. God's Word broke that tradition and my wife, my children, and their children are experiencing God's generational prosperity.

4. BASIC WORLDLY PRINCIPLES

Colossians 2:8 (NLT) states this very well:

> *Don't let anyone capture you with empty philosophies and high-sounding nonsense that come from human thinking and from the spiritual powers of this world, rather than from Christ.*

At large, the world is being governed by spiritual powers that are not of God. They are the antichrist and you and I need to discern them and oppose them with the truth of

God's Word and His kind of love. *The Passion Translation* of Colossians 2:8 excellently states it this way:

> *Beware that no one distracts you or intimidates you in their attempt to lead you away from Christ's fullness by pretending to be full of wisdom when they're filled with endless arguments of human logic. For they operate with humanistic and clouded judgments based on the mindset of this world system, and not the anointed truths of the Anointed One.*
>
> COLOSSIANS 2:8 (TPT)

There are anointed truths that set people free. God's Word reveals these anointed truths that make us a counterculture in this world. God's Word is what sanctifies us and sets us apart from this world (see John 17:17). Only when we let "God be true and every man a liar" are we being the counterculture in this world (see Rom. 3:4).

The counterculture is God's truth rooted in the Holy Scriptures, the teachings of the apostles, and the Holy Spirit leading and guiding us in both thought and deed. This counterculture is based on these unshakable, anointed truths of Jesus Himself.

In short, creating a counterculture begins with *what we believe*, but doesn't end there. It is rooted in *who we believe we are* as the church. It becomes tangible in *how we behave*. I urge you to believe God's Word, receive who you are in Christ, behave in a way that reflects what you believe, and realize the power that Christ has given you to be a light in the darkness.

CHAPTER 3

CULTURE OF HATE

*Anyone who hates another brother
or sister is really a murderer at
heart. And you know that murderers
don't have eternal life within them.*
—1 JOHN 3:15 (NLT)

Hate is a human emotion that is poison to the soul. It is working ill will toward your neighbor and doing harm to one another. Unforgiveness is the root cause of hate. Unresolved hate leads to a life of bitterness that leaves a wake of trouble and destruction. Hebrews 12:15 warns us that any *"root of bitterness springing up cause* **trouble,** *and by this many become* defiled." Unforgiveness is the only poison we drink believing it will kill someone else.

We were not created to carry hate, resentment, or bitterness, and Jesus is very clear that hate in the human heart is a form of murder. It is a type of spiritual suicide and is the death of the human soul.

Love is the counter response to hate. It wants nothing but good. Love can have compassion associated with it but is more of an action than an emotion. In time, love affects our emotions but goes far beyond them. Love is an action of forgiveness and works no ill will toward its neighbor.

> For the commandments, "You shall not commit adultery," "You shall not murder," "You shall not steal," "You shall not bear false witness," "You shall not covet," and if there is any other commandment, are all summed up in this saying, namely, "You shall love your neighbor as yourself." Love does no harm to a neighbor; therefore love is the fulfillment of the law.
>
> ROMANS 13:9-10

Paul is using God's moral law from Exodus 20 to demonstrate what unloving looks like. When we violate this law, we are working "ill will" toward our neighbor.

Love is described here as an action, not a feeling. You may think you love your neighbor's wife and desire to sleep with her, but do you love her husband and children? Will having an affair work ill will to her family? Do you still disagree? Well, let me say it like this: If I love you, I don't sleep with your wife, steal your belongings, or bear false witness against you. I hope that helps!

A scripture regarding child training deals with this concept as well. Hate is manifested through inaction, and in stark contrast, love is born out of action.

> *He that spareth his rod hateth his son: but he that loveth him chasteneth him betimes* [early].
>
> PROVERBS 13:24

This passage is universally misquoted, missing the true meaning and impact. We've all heard "spare the rod and spoil the child." No. The New Living Translation of Proverbs 13:24 reads: "*Those who spare the rod of discipline **hate their children.** Those who* love their children *care enough to discipline them.*"

Notice it's not the rod of "wrath and anger" but of discipline. God's discipline is not abusive, nor is it administered in wrath or anger. However, according to Scripture, when we withhold discipline we actually hate our child. Lovingly disciplining our child when they need it shows we love and care for them. We see that in hate there is no action and in love there is action. There is no mention of feelings.

To allow a child to be raised with no boundaries or concept of personal responsibility for their actions is a form of hate. Another form of hate is for us to neglect teaching our children that there are consequences for their choices, good or bad. We love them by teaching God's moral boundaries and the repercussions for violating those boundaries.

Love doesn't remain silent over sin and its destructive power. Today we're accused of hate speech whenever we warn our neighbor of the wages of sin. In truth, as children of God, we can't condone what God condemns and call it love.

In actuality, to gloss over or justify sin through our silence or inaction would be the truest form of hate speech. Remember, God speaks out when there is danger ahead, so listen.

Leviticus 19:15-18 perfectly outlines God's expectation for each of us when showing love for our neighbor.

> *Do not twist justice in legal matters by favoring the poor or being partial to the rich and powerful. Always judge people fairly. Do not spread slanderous gossip among your people. Do not stand idly by when your neighbor's life is threatened. I am the Lord. Do not nurse hatred in your heart for any of your relatives. Confront people directly so you will not be held guilty for their sin. Do not seek revenge or bear a grudge against a fellow Israelite, but love your neighbor as yourself. I am the Lord.*
>
> LEVITICUS 19: 15-18 (NLT)

Jesus was quoting from this passage in Matthew 22:39, *"love your neighbor as yourself."* It is not love when we ignore sin and refuse to warn people of things that are harmful to them. In fact, we are actually hating them through our silence. When we are afraid to speak the truth in love, we actually love ourselves more than others. Everyone has a right to reject the truth for themselves. We have no right to reject it for them in our silence.

TAUGHT TO HATE

What does a culture of hate look like? Our world today would have you believe that speaking out against its agenda is hate-filled. But what does God say about this?

What sorrow for those who drag their sins behind
them with ropes made of lies, who drag wickedness
behind them like a cart! They even mock God and
say, "Hurry up and do something! We want to see
what you can do. Let the Holy One of Israel carry
out his plan, for we want to know what it is." What
sorrow for those who say that evil is good and good
is evil, that dark is light and light is dark, that bitter
is sweet and sweet is bitter.

ISAIAH 5:18-20 (NLT)

This scripture perfectly reflects God's definition of a culture of hate and speaks directly to our world culture today where everything is absolutely backward and upside down. We are not off-kilter by a few degrees—that's possible for any of us. This is 180 degrees out of phase. Sexual purity is mocked and assailed while all types of perversion are celebrated. Identity-crushing LGBTQA+ indoctrination is defiling the moral innocence of our children. Late-term abortions are celebrated by our leaders. Babies from botched abortions are legally euthanized or left to die. Cities burn in the name of justice. Police are shot and bystanders rejoice. Violence is encouraged by the mainstream media for better ratings. Racism has become an issue of "skin," not sin—up is down and down is up and on and on I could go.

Our courts oppose the righteous, and justice is
nowhere to be found. Truth stumbles in the streets,
and honesty has been outlawed. Yes, truth is gone,
and anyone who renounces evil is attacked. The

> *Lord looked and was displeased to find there was no justice.*
>
> ISAIAH 59:14-15 (NLT)

Because of corruption and hate for truth and God's justice, many of our courts today oppose the righteous and reward the wicked. Honesty has been outlawed in the "cancel culture." Truth is censored, there are bans on social media, and people who are trying to speak truth are de-platformed.

Those who renounce evil and turn from it become targets. Whoever stands for God's justice for all; defends the weakest (babies in the womb); believes in law enforcement, law and order, respect for the flag, or dares to call out black-on-black crime believing that all black lives matter, these people are at risk of being attacked.

Defending the institution of marriage between a man and woman and believing God created us male and female (2 genders, not 57) tags people as bigots, homophobes, sexists, racists, or any other foul name. To sum things up, rage and hate have become the acceptable way of communicating differences and we are, quite literally, being taught to hate one another for any reason.

DIVIDING RIGHT FROM WRONG

The "facts" or "science" as communicated to us seem to be changing daily and drifting further away from God's Kingdom principles. That is why it is paramount to know God's truth concerning every issue we face. It is His Word that rightly divides right from wrong, moral from immoral, up from down, and in from out (see Heb. 4:12; 2 Tim. 3:16-17). God's Word never changes (see Matt. 24:35; Heb. 13:8). God's

Word gives us direction in life. It is the constant foundation we can build our lives on. Try as we might, we can't save ourselves with climate change policies, political correctness, socialism, and communism. These worldly philosophies are destroying and enslaving current and future generations.

> *Your word is a lamp to my feet and a light to my path.*
>
> PSALM 119:105

God's Word brings light and understanding on how to live our lives pleasing to God. It is truth that can bring freedom to our souls from all the darkness of our world. Jesus taught us the power and source of truth and said to those Jews who believed in Him:

> *If you abide in My word, you are My disciples indeed. And you shall know the truth, and the truth shall make you free.*
>
> JOHN 8:31-32

We must *know* truth to be set free. God's truth is found and known by abiding in Christ and His Word that brings freedom. If knowing the truth brings freedom, what do all these lies in our culture bring? The answer is simple—bondage.

We must be a counterculture to all this chaos and confusion, understanding that it is love, not hate, to speak God's Word regarding righteousness, peace, and joy in the Holy Spirit. Our silence for fear of persecution—and in some cases prosecution—is not a sign of godliness. Our fear of offending the wicked and unjust around us has contributed to the deception of the innocent, weak, and immature among us. We must be willing to be persecuted for righteousness' sake (see Matt. 5:11-12). If we do not lovingly push back, the persecution may turn to prosecution and ultimately execution.

President John F. Kennedy paraphrased Edmund Burke's thoughts on the triumph of evil with the famous quote: "The only thing necessary for the triumph of evil is for good men to do nothing." Only the truth of God's Word can save us all from evil and the escalation of hate in our world. God's love is not selfish—His love causes us to care about others and their eternal souls. His love drives us to speak up and stand up against evil.

LOVE

As Christians, our counterculture is a Kingdom culture that is dominated by grace and mercy with God's love as the centerpiece of all discussions. *"Do to others as you would have them do to you"* (Luke 6:31 NIV). This is known as the "Golden Rule." This is what God's love looks like practically. On the other hand, hate does to others what has been done to them in the same evil way it was done. It treats others in the same way they have been treated versus treating others the way they want to be treated.

As a church, we are not to be a culture of "do to others as they have done to you." Rather, we are to be a culture of God's love based on His character, not others' conduct. Our love for one another—even those we disagree with—should be based on the love of God that is shed abroad in our hearts by the Holy Spirit, rather than feelings or emotions (see Rom. 5:5).

The motive behind our counterculture is genuine love for God and one another. We are no longer an *"eye for an eye"* kind of culture. The Passion Translation of Romans 12:19 says, *"Beloved, don't be obsessed with taking revenge, but leave that to God's righteous justice. For the Scriptures say: 'Vengeance is mine, and I will repay' says the Lord."*

A day of God's judgment is coming for rejecting Jesus and His sacrifice for all our sins, but today God is calling us to repentance. Jesus did not come into the world to condemn it, but rather to save it (see John 3:17). In John 3:18 Jesus says, *"He who believes in Him is not condemned; but he who does not believe is condemned already, because he has not believed in the name of the only begotten Son of God."* Unbelief or rejecting Jesus will end in final judgment. That sentence of death (condemnation) was on us all before Christ. Jesus saved us from that when we accepted Him.

While God never condones sin, and neither should we, He does not condemn any of us for our failures and shortcomings. He wants nothing more than for us to allow His love to penetrate our hearts and redeem us. While He does call us to a life of holiness, He understands that it is a process for us to get there. He is always offering forgiveness, redemption, and mercy during the process. He knows that love devoid of redemption is not love at all. Our culture is not just about what we believe but how we treat one another in our journey of faith—how we behave:

> *By this all will know that you are My disciples, if you have love for one another.*
>
> JOHN 13:35

True, healthy love originates from God and is based on who He is (see 1 John 4:7-8). It is unconditional, transformative, and eternal. We can't do anything to get Him to love us more or to love us less. God's love is unoffendable and treats even the worst among us with kindness and long-suffering. We are to treat one another with respect and honor because of God's love:

> But I say, love your enemies! Pray for those who persecute you! In that way, you will be acting as true children of your Father in heaven. For he gives his sunlight to both the evil and the good, and he sends rain on the just and the unjust alike. If you love only those who love you, what reward is there for that? Even corrupt tax collectors do that much. If you are kind only to your friends, how are you different from anyone else? Even pagans do that. But you are to be perfect, even as your Father in heaven is perfect.
> MATTHEW 5:44-48 (NLT)

We are called to model our behavior after our heavenly Father. How God treats people is how we should as His children. His kind of love should be based on our character as well, not people's conduct. We love people regardless of their conduct because of God's love in our hearts.

FEAR

> There is no fear in love, but perfect love casts out fear. For fear has to do with punishment, and whoever fears has not been perfected in love.
> 1 JOHN 4:18 (ESV)

As you can see, when we keep ourselves in God's perfect love, fear is cast out. Because of the cross and sacrifice Jesus made for sin, as believers we have no fear of God's punishment for sin. Jesus bore God's wrath and punishment for sin on the cross. We have no tormenting fear of God as Christians. Our fear of God is reverence and awe at the work of the cross and sacrifice of Jesus for our sins. Not having tormenting or negative fear of God delivers us from the fear of man.

It's important we understand this so we can stand in the face of hate, violence, threats, and any form of persecution for speaking the truth in love. Knowing God's complete forgiveness and mercy for you emboldens you to say the right thing, do the right thing, and do it the right way without fearing persecution, prosecution, or execution. Even the fear of death is defeated in God's love. If God is for us, there should be no fear of those who may be against us (see Rom. 8:31).

LOVE IS TAUGHT

God's kind of love must be taught, not caught. It's not like a virus that comes and goes. You don't fall in or out of it. It is a choice regardless of circumstances, feelings, or how others may be acting. It's not a response to my surroundings, but rather a response to God being inside me. We operate in it by faith and not feelings or emotions. Titus 2:3-4 talks about this principle in relation to older women with experience teaching the younger women certain life skills:

> *The aged women likewise, that they be in behaviour as becometh holiness, not false accusers, not given to much wine, teachers of good things; that they*

may teach the young women to be sober, to love their husbands, to love their children.

TITUS 2:3-4

Notice they had to be taught to love their husbands and children. Scripture teaches that it's the Holy Spirit that teaches us to love. In today's culture we are being told that love is caught and based on feelings rather than something we need to be educated in. I dive more into how God teaches us to love in the next chapter.

But as touching brotherly love ye need not that I write unto you: for ye yourselves are taught of God to love one another.

1 THESSALONIANS 4:9

In a speech given by Martin Luther King, Jr. he said: "Darkness cannot drive out darkness: only light can do that. Hate cannot drive out hate; only love can do that." I believe his words perfectly sum up what our counterculture looks like. We cannot respond to hate with hate or condemn people who are struggling with sin. We are not to be mean-spirited, condescending, or judgmental.

Instead, we are to respond to this world trapped in darkness with forgiveness, mercy, and compassion. We are to boldly declare God's truth and righteousness with gratitude for God's redemptive power in our own lives and be ever willing to extend that same forgiveness to anyone who might hurt us. To create an effective counterculture, we must settle our hearts into the kind of love that hopes, believes, and endures all things (see 1 Cor. 13:7).

CHAPTER 4

CULTURE OF LOVE

*Beloved, let us love one another, for love
is of God; and everyone who loves is born
of God and knows God. He who does not
love does not know God, for God is love.*
—1 JOHN 4:7-8

How do we develop a culture of love? Notice that "love is
of God." Love is not of this world or our flesh. Love is
not of me or my senses; it is of God.
Two things must occur for us to love
each other. One, we must be born of
God; and second, we must know
God. You cannot love by rejecting
God who is love. Being born again is
the beginning of a life filled with

> **WHAT THE
> WORLD CALLS
> LOVE IS NOT
> LOVE AT ALL.**

God's kind of love or having a revelation of God Himself. What the world calls love is not love at all.

First Corinthians 13:4-8 describes God's kind of love—what it looks like, how it acts, or in some cases doesn't act. There are sixteen descriptions of love that are the character and nature of love. One of them is verse 6—love, *"does not rejoice in iniquity."* God's love cannot operate in wrongdoing, but in our world today, sin is openly celebrated and presented as love. The second part of verse 6 says *"but rejoices in the truth."* The counterculture rejoices in God's Word and celebrates truth, not iniquity. God's love is His character and nature, not ours independent of Him.

We cannot give what we don't have, so our ability to love starts when we truly believe and receive God's love. In fact, it is impossible for us to love with God's kind of love until, by faith, we believe it and then receive it for ourselves. We all must experience God's love before we can express it.

John, the apostle of God's kind of love, says in 1 John 4:16-17:

> *And we have known and believed the love that God has for us. God is love, and he who abides in love abides in God, and God in him. Love has been perfected among us in this: that we may have boldness in the day of judgment; because as He is, so are we in this world.*

Notice they knew God loved them and believed it. We receive God's love for us by revelation and faith. Verse 17 says, *"Love has been perfected among us in this."* Perfected in what? Knowing and believing God's love for us! Few believers are walking in God's kind of love because they don't know how much God loves them. Once we come to know it, we must then believe it. It takes faith to believe God loves us the way He truly does. Once we come to "know and believe" we are then able to share it with our neighbors. Verse 17 goes on to say that we will have boldness in the day of judgment and then declares that we are "as Jesus is in this world." This is a reference to our born-again spirit. We are not as Jesus is in our unrenewed minds or our bodies.

Our spirit is the part of us that is righteous and truly holy. It has God's love in it by the Holy Spirit (see Rom. 5:5). There is a day of judgment coming, but because we have believed God's love for us in Jesus, we will have boldness in that day. Because of God's love, we have been forgiven and accepted by God, whereas the world that is abiding in hate will not. I shared in the last chapter how love is *taught, not caught* (see Tit. 2:4).

There are three major ways God has revealed His love and thereby teaches us to love one another:

1. THE HOLY SPIRIT (BY REVELATION)

> *The love of God has been poured out in our hearts*
> *by the Holy Spirit who was given to us.*

> ROMANS 5:5

It is the Holy Spirit in our hearts that reveals God's love. God's kind of love is not like the world's. In the world, love is felt with our senses. God and His kind of love are revealed and then taught to us by the Holy Spirit. Paul is praying for the church at Ephesus, and he asks:

That the God of our Lord Jesus Christ, the Father of glory, may give to you the spirit of wisdom and revelation in the knowledge of Him, the eyes of your understanding being enlightened; that you may know what is the hope of His calling, what are the riches of the glory of His inheritance in the saints.

EPHESIANS 1:17-18

A revelation in the knowledge of Him is one of love. As we grow in revelation of His love for us, we begin to love others the same way.

As we receive His forgiveness, we are then able to forgive. As we see by revelation and receive His mercy, we share it.

But concerning brotherly love you have no need that I should write to you, for you yourselves are taught by God to love one another.

1 THESSALONIANS 4:9

We are taught by God, not man, to love. God may use men as vessels, but it is the Holy Spirit working in and through them that reveals and teaches God's kind of love. Men who do not know God or are not born of Him cannot know love or teach us to love.

God (who is love) is known by the Spirit, not the senses or our carnal unrenewed minds (see Rom. 8:6-7). Second Corinthians 5:7 says, "*we walk by faith and not by sight.*" We know God and please Him by faith, not our emotions or five senses (hearing, smelling, sight, taste, feeling). God is a Spirit and is to be worshiped in spirit and truth (see John 4:24). In Matthew 16:13-17 we see how God is known. Jesus (God's love made flesh) is known by revelation. Revelation is something revealed by God.

When Jesus asked His disciples in Matthew 16:13, *"Who do men say that I, the son of Man, am?"* they gave numerous answers: John, Elijah, etc. Then Jesus asked them in verse 15, *"Who do you say that I am?"* Peter said, *"You are the Christ, the Son of the living God."* Jesus' response to Peter's accurate account was that flesh and blood *did not reveal* this, *"but My Father who is in heaven"* (Matt. 16:17). God revealed to Peter who Jesus is. Jesus is God (love) made flesh (see John 1:14). It's the Holy Spirit who reveals God's love to us. It is known by the Spirit, not the world. When those who have rejected God try to define and explain love, we should understand that it is not God's kind of love or even love at all. Love is of God and *"he who abides in love abides in God"* (1 John 4:16). To reject God is to reject love.

2. THE CROSS

God proved His love for us over two thousand years ago. Love is known by an action that occurred in the past (the cross), not a circumstance of the present. While God is with me in my present, working, moving, and revealing Himself, He has already proven His love for me at the cross. I can never allow my current circumstances to cause me to waver or question God's love.

> *For God so loved the world that He gave His only begotten Son, that whoever believes in Him should not perish but have everlasting life.*
>
> JOHN 3:16

This is a reference to the cross. The giving of Jesus on the cross, for our sins, was God's love for us.

> *But God demonstrates His own love toward us, in that while we were still sinners, Christ died for us [on the cross].*
>
> ROMANS 5:8

To demonstrate is to prove something. The King James Version uses the word *commendeth* (*suristao*, Strong's G4921). *Commend* means to introduce or exhibit, to constitute or approve. God introduced and exhibited to the world at the cross a love never known or seen.

> *By this we know love, because He laid down His life for us. And we also ought to lay down our lives for the brethren.*
>
> 1 JOHN 3:16

The cross reveals God's love in that while we had rejected God and His love, Jesus died for us. While we were yet sinners and enemies of God, Christ died for us. That's unconditional, unmerited love. We did not earn or deserve that kind of sacrifice. Even today God's love initiates first in character and virtue, not in response to our conduct or defects. When our senses betray us, the Holy Spirit reveals the cross. The trials and afflictions we go through are designed by Satan to separate us from God's love and to create doubt in the steadfast love of Christ.

Satan will always tempt you to look to your circumstances and feelings to discern God's love by giving you thoughts like, *If God loves you why is this happening? If God loves you, why did you lose your child, your job, your spouse?* He tempts us to discern God's love in the light of the present circumstances versus the proof of the past—*the cross*. Even though the apostle Paul went through a lot of trials, tribulations, and hardships, he was able to overcome all his persecutions and hardships because he knew and believed God's love for him.

> *For I am persuaded that neither death nor life, nor angels nor principalities nor powers, nor things present nor things to come, nor height nor depth, nor any other created thing, shall be able to separate us from the love of God which is in Christ Jesus our Lord.*
>
> ROMANS 8:38-39

Many today are simply not persuaded. As we yield to the Holy Spirit, He will reveal to us the cross. What Jesus did for us at the cross will persuade you of God's love. First Corinthians 1:18, "*For the message of the cross is foolishness to those who are perishing, but to us who are being saved it is the power of God.*" God's love revealed in the cross is God's power to save us.

3. THE WORD: BOTH LIVING (JESUS) AND WRITTEN (SCRIPTURES)

> *And the Word became flesh and dwelt among us, and we beheld His glory, the glory as of the only begotten of the Father, full of grace and truth.*
>
> JOHN 1:14

Jesus reveals God who is love (see 1 John 3:8). Jesus was God made flesh or God with eyeballs and hands. In 1 John 1:1, John spoke of the Word they had heard and seen. The New Living Translation puts it like this: "*We saw him with our own eyes and touched him with our own hands."* The writer of Hebrews makes it very plain and clear who Jesus is:

> *Who being the brightness of His glory and the express image of His person, and upholding all things by the word of His power, when He had by Himself purged our sins, sat down at the right hand of the Majesty on high.*
>
> HEBREWS 1:3

Christ is the brightness of God's glory and express image of His person. He didn't reveal just a part of God or some of God, He revealed all of God. He was the physical, tangible image of God:

> *Christ is the visible image of the invisible God.*
>
> COLOSSIANS 1:15 (NLT)

In John 14:7, Jesus said to His disciples, *"If you had known Me, you would have known My Father also; and from now on you know Him and have seen Him."* Verse 9 says, *"He who has seen Me has seen the Father."* We can be assured that God loves people because Christ loved people. As you go back through Scripture, you will see that Jesus consistently warned people of the dangers of sin and upcoming judgment, but He never condemned them.

A fitting example of this is found in John 8. The Pharisees caught a woman in the act of adultery. After bringing her to Jesus, they demanded that she be stoned according to the Law of Moses. Jesus knelt next to the woman briefly and said, *"All right, but let the one who has never sinned throw the first stone"* (John 8:7 NLT). A hush fell over the crowd and then: *"When the accusers heard this, they slipped away one by one, beginning with the oldest, until only Jesus was left in the middle of the crowd with the woman"* (John 8:9 NLT).

No one was sinless but Jesus. He could have judged her but extended God's mercy instead. When the Pharisees and mob left the scene, John 8:10 (NLT) says:

> *Then Jesus stood up again and said to the woman, "Where are your accusers? Didn't even one of them condemn you?" "No, Lord," she said. And Jesus said, "Neither do I. Go and sin no more."*

Why did Jesus say He didn't condemn her either? Because He was the only one without sin and therefore qualified to stone her. He could have but chose to extend love and mercy with an admonition to "go and sin no more." This is God's love that leads to redemption. A love that celebrates and glorifies sin is not God's love. His love releases us from sin to serve Him and not our flesh.

In John 5, Jesus heals a lame man. He later finds the man in the temple and tells him in verse 14: *"Now you are well; so stop sinning, or something even worse may happen to you"* (NLT). We create a counterculture of love when we extend grace and mercy with a warning to "sin no more" rather than condemnation.

LOVE WARNS OF DANGER

In addition to ministering to people, the disciples were instructed to preach the gospel in the cities surrounding Jerusalem. They were to stay in a home and share the good news of God's love. If it was a worthy house and receptive to the gospel, they were to leave their peace upon it. If not, their peace was to return to them.

> *And whosoever shall not receive you, nor hear your words, when ye depart out of that house or city, shake off the dust of your feet. Verily I say unto you, It shall be more tolerable for the land of Sodom and Gomorrha in the day of judgment, than for that city.*
> MATTHEW 10:14-15

Remember, saints, this was Love speaking. Jesus operated perfectly in God's love. If people rejected the gospel spoken to them then judgment would one day come. When people reject the Scriptures, they are rejecting God Himself. Jesus spoke of the coming judgment on the city of Capernaum for rejecting Him:

> *And you, Capernaum, who are exalted to heaven, will be brought down to Hades; for if the mighty works which were done in you had been done in Sodom, it would have remained until this day. But I say to you that it shall be more tolerable for the land of Sodom in the day of judgment than for you.*
> MATTHEW 11:23-24

He warned Chorazin and Bethsaida of the same in verses 21 and 22 of that same chapter.

Luke speaks of Lot's departure from Sodom and the destruction that came:

> *But the same day that Lot went out of Sodom it rained fire and brimstone from heaven, and*

*destroyed them all. Even thus shall it be in the day
when the Son of man is revealed.*

LUKE 17:29-30

A day of fire and brimstone is coming. We must repent
and be saved from the wrath to come. This is what Christians are saved from (see Rom. 5:9). This is not hate speech
from Jesus, but rather God's love and desire to save us from
the wrath to come. At one point John the Baptist warned a
crowd at the River Jordan of the coming wrath:

> *When the crowds came to John for baptism, he said,
> "You brood of snakes! Who warned you to flee the
> coming wrath?"*

LUKE 3:7 (NLT)

Was that wrong to warn them of a wrath that will one
day come? No, it was love! In today's church culture, if you
even bring up sin, issues of sin, or the dangers of sin and
rebellion to God, you are considered unloving. Jesus was
Love manifest in the flesh and yet He called out the Pharisees of His day:

> *What sorrow awaits you teachers of religious law
> and you Pharisees. Hypocrites! For you are like
> whitewashed tombs—beautiful on the outside but
> filled on the inside with dead people's bones and all
> sorts of impurity.*

MATTHEW 23:27 (NLT)

Jesus is warning them of coming judgment if they remain
in their present condition. We must all be honest about sin in
our own lives and quick to repent. We must also be merciful
and point people to the love of God in Christ Jesus our Lord.

Jesus confronted sin but offered comfort to the sinner. He did not ignore, minimize, or cover up the dangers of sin, but always extended forgiveness. He constantly revealed our sin to show us our need for repentance and forgiveness. We must expose the darkness of this world with the motive to bring people to the light. Faith in Jesus saves us from the wrath to come—receiving God's love and forgiveness. The apostle Paul maintained an honest and humble spirit regarding sin. *"This is a faithful saying and worthy of all acceptance, that Christ Jesus came into the world to save sinners, **of whom I am chief**"* (1 Tim. 1:15). He had no self-righteousness in his heart; he was thankful for God's love in saving him. We are to be forever grateful for God's mercy on us and thereby extend such mercy to others.

This counterculture of love is God's Kingdom culture! It is dominated by Kingdom principles. It must be led by the Holy Spirit. It is filled with forgiveness and redemptive truth that leads to reconciliation with God and one another. We must preach the cross, which is the power of God for salvation, and live out God's Word showing loyalty to Jesus above anyone else. God's Holy Spirit teaches us what love is and how to love. It is on the cross that God demonstrated His love for us. It is His word both living (Jesus) and written (Scriptures) that teaches us God's kind of love.

CHAPTER 5

CULTURE OF DEATH

The thief does not come except to steal, and to kill, and to destroy. I have come that they may have life, and that they may have it more abundantly.
—JOHN 10:10

If it steals, kills, or destroys, it is not God. We don't need a forensic team to understand that. These are the fingerprints of Satan's culture.

On the other hand, God's counterculture is life and Jesus is here to give us that life in abundance. Over the past few years, we've seen the news dominated with pandemic hysteria, vaccine controversy, election chaos, violence in the streets, terrorism, lawlessness, and the list goes on.

Who can forget when a Minneapolis police officer grossly mishandled the arrest of a civilian named

George Floyd? It was a brutal, ungodly act that resulted in the loss of life. The response nationwide was one of outrage and anger, as it should have been. While this demanded justice, vicious attacks against the police and mob rule were not the answer. Vigilantism was not, and will never be, justice. There is absolutely no justification for what we witnessed. Death and darkness appear to be dominant forces at work in our culture today. The absence of God's kind of life has created a black hole for death.

> *There is a path before each person that seems right,*
> *but it ends in death.*
> PROVERBS 16:25 (NLT)

It's the path of hate, anger, deceit, and violence that always leads to death and all its many forms. When one takes that literal dead-end road, he drags his family, friends, and neighbors along with him on a dark journey. In Genesis 6:11 it says, *"The earth also was corrupt before God, and the earth was filled with violence."* Any path that seems right in human eyes will eventually corrupt everything it touches and end in violence. This was the condition of humankind on the earth leading to the great flood.

> *The Lord saw that the wickedness of man was*
> *great in the earth, and that every intention of the*
> *thoughts of his heart was only evil continually. And*
> *the Lord regretted that he had made man on the*
> *earth, and it grieved him to his heart. So the Lord*
> *said, "I will blot out man whom I have created from*
> *the face of the land, man and animals and creeping*
> *things and birds of the heavens, for I am sorry that I*

*have made them." But Noah found favor in the eyes
of the Lord.*

GENESIS 6:5-8 (ESV)

Noah and his family were the only ones standing against the culture of death and violence. We must be willing to stand in these challenging times and find favor in the Lord's eyes.

When God made Adam and Eve, He was very pleased with Creation. However, it wasn't long before they disobeyed God by doing what seemed right to them and partook of the forbidden fruit. Because of their disobedience, they had to leave the Garden of Eden.

From Adam to Noah the earth eroded into violence and had to be cleansed. God saw the righteousness of Noah and his family and devised a plan to rid the world of evil and create the sanctuary He had always wanted for mankind. He helped Noah build an ark that housed him, his family, and two of every kind of creature on the earth. For forty days and nights, the earth was consumed by rain.

After the waters subsided, the ark was emptied and God commanded every living creature to multiply, filling the earth once again. He put a rainbow in the sky as His promise to never flood the earth again because of sin.

As the years went by, the people once again began to do evil in the sight of the Lord. He then set apart a people unto Himself (the seed of Abraham) and gave them the Law of Moses clearly defining right and wrong. It was also given to put a restraint on sin in the heart of man. We all know it at its most basic form as the Ten Commandments, which counter death and reflect what life and love look like. Found in Exodus 20:3-17, these Ten Commandments are God's moral law (see Exod. 20:3-17).

1. You shall have no other gods before Me.

2. You shall not bow down to them nor serve them.

3. You shall not take the name of the Lord thy God in vain.

4. Remember the Sabbath and keep it holy.

5. Honor your father and mother.

6. You shall not murder.

7. You shall not commit adultery.

8. You shall not steal.

9. You shall not bear false witness against your neighbor.

10. You shall not covet.

These Ten Commandments put a restraint on hate, violence, and death. Obedience to these is life. It is what love for God and each other looks like. However, with this Law came wrath, curses, and punishment for sin. Over time people continued doing what was right in their own eyes, falling further into depravity. Knowing this would happen, God had a plan:

> *For God so loved the world that He gave His only begotten Son, that whoever believes in Him should not perish but have everlasting life.*
> JOHN 3:16

Christ, the Son of God, came into the world to redeem us from the wrath, curses, and punishment for sin. His sacrifice on the cross paid the ransom on our heads. With faith in Jesus Christ came eternal life. Through faith in the cross, we are forgiven of our sins and given a new heart with God's love in it. In the counterculture, it is God's love that puts a restraint on sin and evil. We now have the law written in our hearts and it restrains us from working any ill will toward our neighbor (see Rom. 5:5; 13:10; 2 Cor. 5:14).

If a man rejects Christ, then all there is to restrain him is the law—civil law rooted in God's moral law. Paul told Timothy in 1 Timothy 1:8-9, *"We know that the law is good if one uses it lawfully, knowing this: that the law is not made for a righteous person."* As you can see, Paul said that the law *is not* made for a righteous person. Before we talk about exactly who the law *is* made for, let's start by finding out how the Bible defines a righteous person:

> *For He made Him who knew no sin to be sin for us, that we might become the righteousness of God in Him.*
>
> 2 CORINTHIANS 5:21

> *For as by one man's disobedience many were made sinners, so also by one Man's obedience, many will be made righteous.*
>
> ROMANS 5:19

> *And that you put on the new man which was created according to God, in true righteousness and holiness.*
>
> EPHESIANS 4:24

In short, the Law of Moses was not made for those who have earnestly chosen Christ, confessed Him as Lord, and ultimately been born again being made righteous and truly holy. So, who is it for?

> *For the lawless and insubordinate, for the ungodly and for sinners, for the unholy and profane, for murderers of fathers and murderers of mothers, for manslayers, for fornicators, for sodomites, for kidnappers, for liars, for perjuries, and if there is any other thing that is contrary to sound doctrine, according to the glorious gospel of the blessed God which was committed to my trust.*
>
> 1 TIMOTHY 1:9-11

The law was given to reveal our sin and drive us to faith in Christ. It revealed our need and drove us to the solution to our fallen condition—Jesus and the cross. It put a restraint on sin for the rebellious and disobedient.

The law was made to constrain anyone who has not accepted the gospel of Christ and been made holy by His indwelling Spirit. Likewise, civil law is to put a restraint on evil or else one suffers harsh penalties or imprisonment.

> *Let every soul be subject to the governing authorities. For there is no authority except from God, and the authorities that exist are appointed by God. Therefore whoever resists the authority resists the ordinance of God, and those who resist will bring judgment on themselves. For rulers are not a terror to good works, but to evil. ...But if you do evil, be afraid; for he does not bear the sword in vain; for*

he is God's minister, an avenger to execute wrath on him who practices evil.

Don't misunderstand me—both those who are in Christ and those who are in the world are subject to civil law. (*"Let every soul be subject to the governing authorities."*) If a Christian breaks civil law, they are subject to the consequences as well. If those in government or in law enforcement break the law, they too are held accountable. However, because of the new life of Christ shed abroad in our hearts as believers, there is a restraint on sin from within. Civil law is ordained by God to put a restraint on those who choose death of any kind. While law enforcement must be held accountable in a just and moral society, they stand between the people and total chaos in a culture of death.

All sin is death at work. The love of God shown at the cross brings eternal life. Ultimately, the appearing of Jesus and His Kingdom will be the end of death and its corruption of the human heart and body. Until then, man is given a choice of death or life. So, which will it be—a culture of death (law) or the counterculture of life (love)?

Israel was given a choice by God:

See, I have set before you today life and good, death and evil, in that I command you today to love the Lord your God, to walk in His ways, and to keep His commandments, His statutes, and His judgments, that you may live and multiply; and the Lord your God will bless you in the land which you go to possess. But if your heart turns away so that you do not hear, and are drawn away, and worship other gods and serve them, I announce to you today that you shall surely perish; you shall not prolong your days in the land which you cross over the Jordan to go in and possess. I call heaven and earth as witnesses today against you, that I have set before you life and death, blessing and cursing; therefore choose life, that both you and your descendants may live; that you may love the Lord your God, that you may obey His voice, and that you may cling to Him, for He is your life and the length of your days.

DEUTERONOMY 30:15-20

While this is profound in the way we think of death and life, it really is simple. Death is not just an event where we leave our bodies and meet God, but a choice of obedience or disobedience. Faith obedience to God and His Word equals life. Disobedience and unbelief equal death. For example, it was Adam's disobedience to God's Word that caused him to bring a form of death into the earth right away and that led to his physical death hundreds of years later:

Then the Lord God took the man and put him in the garden of Eden to tend and keep it. And the Lord God commanded the man, saying, "Of every tree of the garden you may freely eat; but of the tree of the knowledge of good and evil you shall not eat, for in the day that you eat of it you shall surely die."

GENESIS 2:15-17

Adam lived to be 930 years of age before he died physically. However, death became a part of his existence the day he disobeyed God. There was a death in his spirit that led to a world of hate and violence. You can see death working in his two sons when Cain kills Abel (see Gen. 4:1-12).

Death can mean separation. James 2:26 says, *"For as the body without the spirit is dead, so faith without works is dead also."* Physical death is your spirit separating from the body. Adam experienced spiritual death in the day he ate of the forbidden tree. There was a spiritual separation from God that allowed death to dominate him and his family. Ultimately, the family of man (all of us) experienced that death. Man's disobedience to God is this culture of death we see today.

> *But now, as to whether there will be a resurrection of the dead—haven't you ever read about this in the Scriptures? Long after Abraham, Isaac, and Jacob had died, God said, "I am the God of Abraham, the God of Isaac, and the God of Jacob." So he is the God of the living, not the dead.*
>
> MATTHEW 22:31-32 (NLT)

Obedience to God is choosing life, even life after our physical death. Jesus speaks of three dead people—Abraham, Isaac, and Jacob—and says they are the living. Even after physical death, they were among the living because of faith in God and obedience to His Word.

CHOOSE LIFE

In contrast, Paul wrote young Timothy regarding widows and the church's responsibility in ministering to them and made a profound statement:

Now she who is really a widow, and left alone, trusts in God and continues in supplications and prayers night and day. But she who lives in pleasure is dead while she lives.

1 TIMOTHY 5:5-6

How could this woman, who was alive, be regarded by Paul as dead? People without God and in disobedience to God are dead inside while appearing alive outside:

And you He made alive, who were dead in trespasses and sins, in which you once walked according to the course of this world, according to the prince of the power of the air, the spirit who now works in the sons of disobedience.

EPHESIANS 2:1-2

Before faith in Christ, we were all dead in our sins and trespasses. Now we've been made alive in Christ. Faith in and obedience to God has brought life to us. Disobedience is death in the world. So, if death can be present even while our bodies are living, what leads to living a dead life?

There are six things the Lord hates—no, seven things he detests: haughty eyes, a lying tongue, hands that kill the innocent, a heart that plots evil, feet that race to do wrong, a false witness who pours out lies, a person who sows discord in a family.

PROVERBS 6:16-19 (NLT)

These are known in some circles as the seven *deadly* sins.

1. Haughty eyes

2. A lying tongue

3. Hands that kill the innocent

4. A heart that plots evil

5. Feet that race to do wrong

6. A false witness who pours out lies

7. A person who sows discord in a family

These are seven deadly sins according to God and He hates them. In the New Living Translation, Romans 12:9 states, *"Don't just pretend to love others. Really love them."* How? *"Hate what is wrong. Hold tightly to what is good."*

All of these things are in disobedience to God and embrace the culture of death. If we want to live the kind of life Christ desires for us, we must stay away from them. The culture of death celebrates these seven character traits of death. These consume a culture that rejects God.

A culture of life celebrates every stage of our lives. All life is sacred and of high value to God. It should be to us as well. To obey is life; to disobey, death. I wonder how many people were in favor of removing the Ten Commandments from our schools and other public places, including courthouses? By doing that we have told entire generations to choose death.

The culture of death celebrates and embraces hate, violence, and harm. It is a culture devoid of God and filled with disobedience to Him and His Word. The culture of life celebrates and embraces God's love and peace. It works no ill toward its neighbor and is in union with Christ, delighting in faith obedience to Jesus.

CHAPTER 6

ORIGINS OF LIFE

There are two primary views of the origins of life—a secular view and a biblical view. The secular view is called the Theory of Evolution. It basically believes we are here by accident and happenstance. This view was popularized by Charles Darwin way back in 1859, and it promotes the idea that humans began as single-celled organisms and evolved over billions of years into our present condition. We went from goo, to the zoo, to you.

If true, this theory releases us from accountability for our actions. If there is no God, then I'm my own boss (god). Then everything good or bad in my life is part of human evolution (happenstance). It releases us from final judgment (accountability) for how we treated one another (justice). There would be no final day of judgment (Great White Throne). This way of thinking gives place for a life of greed, pleasure, and covetousness because, after all, this is all there is. Obviously, this is atheism at its root and embraces death.

A biblical worldview is one of divine design with a Creator God and is obviously based on the biblical account of Creation. Adam was the first man created in God's image and likeness. He was created fully mature and crowned with glory and honor (see Gen. 1:26-27; Ps. 8:5). We did not evolve to where we are today; we have devolved. In a culture of death, man has very little of God's image in him. Hate, death, and darkness have made him, at times, less than human. To be fully human one must have God's love, life, and light in his heart. This is what Jesus came and died for on the cross: to fully forgive us of our sins and restore our fellowship with God by reflecting His glory in the earth once again. To embrace life is to be fully human. God's life is God returning to man His very image and likeness again.

What does God's Word say regarding the origin of life? A culture of life would begin where life begins. This subject alone is worthy of an entire book and more, but let me just highlight a few scriptures that show us God's opinion on the matter:

> *You made all the delicate, inner parts of my body and knit me together in my mother's womb. Thank you for making me so wonderfully complex! Your workmanship is marvelous—how well I know it. You watched me as I was being formed in utter seclusion, as I was woven together in the dark of the womb. You saw me before I was born. Every day of*

my life was recorded in your book. Every moment was laid out before a single day had passed.
PSALM 139:13-16 (NLT)

The Passion Translation gives a beautiful restating of David's words:

You formed my innermost being, shaping my delicate inside and my intricate outside, and wove them all together in my mother's womb. I thank you, God, for making me so mysteriously complex! ...You even formed every bone in my body when you created me in the secret place...Before I'd ever seen the light of day, the number of days you planned for me were already recorded in your book.

Just like David, it is God who forms us in our mother's womb. He believes that each of us is wonderfully and marvelously breathtaking.

Jeremiah the prophet declares his origins and calling from God.

Then the word of the Lord came to me, saying: "Before I formed you in the womb I knew you; before you were born I sanctified you; I ordained you a prophet to the nations."
JEREMIAH 1:4-5

God saw Jeremiah (knew him) before he was in his mother's womb. While yet still in his mother's womb, God ordained him to be a prophet. God's will and plan does not start at birth, but rather in the womb for each of us. God's hand and plan were at work in our mother's womb.

Paul expressed these same revelations of God and His hand on us in the womb: *"But even **before I was born**, God chose me and called me by his marvelous grace"* (Gal. 1:15 NLT). So God forms us, calls us, and has a plan for us in our mother's womb. Many mistakenly believe we came from our parents. We come from God through our parents. We are co-laborers together with God in bringing children into the world. Genesis 25:21-23 states:

> *And Rebekah his wife conceived. And the children struggled together within her: and she said, If it be so, why am I thus? And she went to enquire of the Lord. And the Lord said unto her, Two nations are in thy womb, and two manner of people shall be separated from thy bowels; and the one people shall be stronger than the other people; and the elder shall serve the younger.*

Clearly these boys were human while living in their mother's womb. God's plan for them and the nations that would come from them was declared while they were yet in the womb. Esau was the elder and Jacob the younger. Jacob was the greater and God was later known as the God of Abraham, Isaac, and Jacob. Isaiah declares in chapter 49:

> *The Lord called me from the womb, from the body of my mother he named my name...he who formed me from the womb to be his servant, to bring Jacob back to him.*
>
> ISAIAH 49:1,5 (ESV)

> *From my mother's womb you have been my God.*
>
> PSALM 22:10 (ESV)

DEHUMANIZING VICTIMS

During the national debate in 1973, abortion was discussed only in the light of "a woman's right to her own body." However, the topic of abortion should be more about a baby's right to life.

Nevertheless, during the debate, the public was falsely promised that abortion would be rare, safe, and legal. As it turns out, two of those promises were lies and one was a deception. It has been almost 50 years since abortion was legalized, and more than 62 million babies have been murdered since then in the United States. It is clear that abortions are not rare, nor safe, and legality does not always equate with morality.

All genocide begins with dehumanizing its intended victims. At one point in human history, the abominable practice of slavery was legal worldwide. The argument for slavery then was, "They are less than human." That sounds familiar to me as people today say a baby is just a fetus or tissue mass, not human. Remember the spirit of darkness has been around for thousands of years. These justifications for evil never change.

We need to go back no further than Nazi Germany in the 1940s. No one knows for certain how many lives were exterminated during that time. Most documents were destroyed by the Nazis to cover up their hideous crimes against humanity. It is said that well over six million Jews alone were killed, and the twisted justification for this was they were *inferior* to the German population.

God's Word is the final authority on human life and how we are to relate to one another in the gift of life. All our rights under God in the culture of life are subject to the rights of others. If any of my rights violate yours, then that right can become not only selfish, but sinful. A child's right to life cannot become null and void because of a woman's right to her own body. We have a right to our bodies until we conceive another life within the womb. Those were the arguments of the times. God's Word violates those as well as pure science. Modern technology has advanced and caught up with God's Word confirming life in the womb through the marvel of an ultrasound that clearly reveals the beating heart of a living baby. This technology was not available in 1973, but God's Word was.

The story of John the Baptist in the first chapter of Luke is amazing. The Bible says that John's parents were both righteous in the sight of the Lord, but childless and very old. One day when John's father, Zechariah, was attending to his duties in the temple an angel appeared to him and said:

> Do not be afraid, Zacharias, for your prayer is heard; and your wife Elizabeth will bear you a son, and you shall call his name John. And you will have joy and gladness, and many will rejoice at his birth. For he will be great in the sight of the Lord, and shall drink neither wine nor strong drink. He will also be filled with the Holy Spirit, even from his mother's womb.
>
> LUKE 1:13-15

Did you catch that? The angel said that John the Baptist would be filled with the Holy Spirit, *even from his mother's womb!* God doesn't fill tissue masses with His Spirit. He fills our sons and daughters (see Acts 2:16-18).

In the counterculture, the origin of life begins in the womb. Therefore, life in the womb is sacred and to be defended. The weakest, most defenseless among us are to be preserved. How can any person, preacher, or parish defend abortion? How can we willingly support politicians or any political party that supports and celebrates the shedding of innocent blood? Only in a culture of death could such a crime against humanity be committed.

You might be reading this and thinking this is condemning of women. God forbid. That's the tactic used today to silence the truth. In a counterculture of love, God condemns the act yet extends forgiveness and redemption to the person. While God never condemns us for our mistakes, He never condones sin. He doesn't condemn the men who have forced women to get an abortion as well. Many men use abortion as an escape to have sex with no consequences. God doesn't condemn families that have forced daughters to have an abortion because of shame and dishonor. His forgiveness and mercy are available for all of us who have fallen short of His glory, which includes all of us (see Rom. 3:23-24).

The counterculture of life is not one of imposing guilt or shame on fallen man, but of loving them enough to speak the truth in love to set them free. No matter how uncomfortable things may get, the counterculture cannot be silent over this issue. There are no excuses acceptable to God for our refusal to speak the truth in love. God is a loving, forgiving God and His goodness and mercy are available for all who repent of any sin and receive His goodness.

In Luke 1:26-38, we read the account of the angel Gabriel appearing to the virgin Mary and revealing to her how she will have a baby. He goes on to explain who this baby would be, and that His name would be Jesus. He explained how this would be supernatural by the hand of the Holy Spirit. She eventually believed and then conceived the holy child Jesus, the Son of God. Jesus was the Son of God at conception, not after He was born. God was made flesh in Mary's womb, not after His birth. She now wants to share the good news of her coming child from God with her relative Elizabeth, who was barren, but now miraculously is six months pregnant with John the Baptist.

> *Now Mary arose in those days and went into the hill country with haste, to a city of Judah, and entered the house of Zacharias and greeted Elizabeth. And it happened, when Elizabeth heard the greeting of Mary, that the babe leaped in her womb: and Elizabeth was filled with the Holy Spirit.*
>
> LUKE 1:39-41

Notice how at six months John could hear Mary's voice. He discerned her good news! Elizabeth prophesies in verse 44, saying, *"For indeed, as soon as the voice of your greeting sounded in my ears, **the babe leaped in my womb for joy.**"* Joy is a human emotion.

Abortion is a part of the culture of death. Pro-life is the culture of life. These things are not just political—they are at the very heart of God. God loves children. Very few people even know the Scriptures I've shared on life in the womb.

If we can harden our hearts to the point of shedding innocent blood, what horrors will the culture of death bring in the future? What unintended consequences are we creating for future generations? Part of the great awakening will be a return to the sanctity of human life, from the womb to the tomb. The moral conscience of the nation must be awakened because this is at the heart of the counterculture and goes to the core of the great commandment:

> *"You shall love the Lord your God with all your heart, with all your soul, and with all your mind." This is the first and great commandment. And the second is like it: "You shall love your neighbor as yourself."*
>
> MATTHEW 22:37-39

Babies are included as neighbors we are to love as ourselves. Why is this important? I mentioned slavery earlier on purpose. Today it's hard to believe such a crime against humanity could have occurred. Slavery was a sin of the world abiding in darkness. It was accepted and ignored by the masses for a host of reasons. The Second Great Awakening in the early 19th century (1795–1835) quickened consciences, leading to the Civil War that ended slavery in the United States. Slavery went from a common sin of the world to unacceptable in America.

How did that happen? Ministers Charles Finney, Lyman Beecher, Timothy Dwight, Barton W. Stone, George Whitefield, and the Methodist "circuit riders" were among many Christian leaders preaching truth during that time. Preachers of every protestant church were sharing the gospel, and spiritual revival ultimately reformed our society. The church was awakened by the thunder in pulpits across America. The revelation of "all men created equal" comes from God (light), not darkness. Loving your neighbor as yourself and doing unto others as you would have them do unto you comes from light, not darkness. All the concepts of freedom and liberty originate in light and are hated by darkness.

Abortion is not just about abortion. It's about generations that have accepted the taking of innocent life with no remorse and the hardening of the human heart in darkness. It's about celebrating and embracing darkness—calling evil good and good evil. While the opposition can be intense at times, the abolitionists—those who were against slavery—in the 1800s were also hated by the darkness. As children of light, we can never be comfortable with darkness, and I assure you that darkness will never be comfortable with light.

We judge previous generations for their gross darkness in disrespecting humanity while defending and celebrating our disregard for human life today. The same gospel that broke the darkness then is breaking the darkness now and will continue to do so as people rise up and proclaim the truth according to God's Word!

CHAPTER 7

CULTURE OF DARKNESS

Even if our gospel message is veiled, it is only veiled to those who are perishing, for their minds have been blinded by the god of this age, leaving them in unbelief. Their blindness keeps them from seeing the dayspring light of the gospel of the glory of Christ, who is the divine image of God.
—2 CORINTHIANS 4:3-4 (TPT)

Satan is the god of this world. He has created a culture of darkness that enables the cultures of hate and death to thrive. His culture is filled with deception and lies. He blinds people's minds from the truth with lies and deception, locking them into a place of self-loathing and self-destruction. The blindness we see today is supernatural. People are losing their minds and it is not natural. It takes help to be as wrong as many people are today in their thinking.

Whoever *hates* what God loves and loves what God hates is in darkness. To reject Christ the Light is to embrace darkness, hell itself. Whoever accepts Christ, the Light, becomes a child of light and embraces the counterculture of God's Kingdom. John puts it this way:

> And the judgment is based on this fact: God's light came into the world, but people loved the darkness more than the light, for their actions were evil.
>
> JOHN 3:19 (NLT)

The entire world lies in darkness. If darkness is embraced by rejecting the light, then there is no other place but "outer darkness." To embrace darkness is to celebrate sin and unbelief. It is to refuse to repent and turn to God for salvation. Within the culture of light, there is a willingness to acknowledge sin, repent, and with God's help and amazing grace turn away from it. Those of the light may fall or stumble into darkness but are quick to repent. Those of the darkness live in, love, and celebrate the darkness, refusing to repent. Jesus is the Light of the world, and people rejected that Light because they loved darkness resulting in eternal consequences.

Jesus reveals God to us, delivering us from the power of darkness. Through a revelation of Him, we know God. Spoken in love, our message turns people from darkness to light, breaking the power of Satan and revealing the glory of God.

> *The people that walked in darkness have seen a great light; they that dwell in the land of the shadow of death, upon them hath the light shined.*
>
> ISAIAH 9:2

God passionately desires to bring light into the darkness. He wills to deliver us from the power of darkness and translate us into the Kingdom of His dear Son (see Col. 1:13). Jesus is that great Light that is shining in the land of the shadow of death.

THE PRESENCE OF DARKNESS

While Jesus has delivered us from the *power* of darkness, it is important to know that we are still in the *presence* of darkness. In Psalm 23:5, David is thanking God for preparing a table for him in the presence of his enemies.

In Ephesians 6, Paul speaks of this ongoing battle with darkness. He encourages believers to put on God's armor for this battle and then lays out how to wrestle properly in warfare. Our battle is not with flesh and blood, or people, but with *"principalities, against powers, against the rulers of the* **darkness** *of this world, against* **spiritual wickedness** *in high places"* (Eph. 6:12). I'll break down and explain God's armor in the next chapter.

In Isaiah 42:6-7, the prophet speaks of a light to the gentiles and how God:

> *Called thee in righteousness, and will hold thine hand, and will keep thee, and give thee for a covenant of the people, for a light of the Gentiles; to open the blind eyes, to bring out the prisoners from*

the prison, and them that sit in darkness out of the prison house.

Luke 4:18 shows us a part of God's call and mission for Jesus: "*to proclaim liberty to the captives, and recovery of sight to the blind, to set at liberty those who are oppressed.*" Darkness is the oppressor of the masses and Jesus is the deliverer.

> *God sent a man, John the Baptist, to tell about the light so that everyone might believe because of his testimony. John himself was not the light; he was simply a witness to tell about the light. The one who is the true light, who gives light to everyone, was coming into the world.*
>
> JOHN 1:6-9 (NLT)

Jesus is the Light that is the glory of God. There is no light in this dark world independent of Jesus. Without Him we sit in darkness, bound to it by demons who are chained to it (see 2 Pet. 2:4). Satan can only work in darkness where God has bound him.

> *The Father who has qualified us to be partakers of the inheritance of the saints in the light. He has delivered us from the power of darkness and conveyed us into the kingdom of the Son of His love.*
>
> COLOSSIANS 1:12-13

As believers, we have partaken of an inherited light. We have been delivered from the power of darkness and are not bound by it any longer. We are called and anointed by God to expose and expel darkness as well as walk and live in the light. Again, it's not just a choice we make or refuse. Rather, it's a new identity born in our spirit as light bearers in a dark world. The apostle Peter proclaims this new condition with boundless joy.

> *But you are a chosen generation, a royal priesthood,*
> *a holy nation, His own special people, that you may*
> *proclaim the praises of Him who called you out of*
> *darkness into His marvelous light.*
>
> 1 PETER 2:9

This is part of our new identity in Christ, "a royal priesthood." The priest of the Old Covenant represented God before the people and the people before God. Today as a "holy nation," Jesus is the High Priest giving us a direct line of communication with God through the Holy Spirit. We are priests in the New Covenant, and we offer up to God bloodless sacrifices of worship and thanksgiving now, as well as prayers for others. We are one nation in Jesus, and all the divisions of flesh are torn down. Notice again, we are "called out of darkness into His marvelous light." Jesus said He came as "*a light into the world, that whosoever believeth on me should* ***not abide in darkness***" (John 12:46).

In speaking and witnessing to King Agrippa, Paul shared why God sent him to the Gentiles:

> *To open their eyes, in order to turn them from dark-*
> *ness to light, and from the power of Satan to God,*
> *that they may receive forgiveness of sins and an*
> *inheritance among those who are sanctified by*
> *faith in Me* [Jesus].
>
> ACTS 26:18

Paul declares in Ephesians 5:8, "*ye were sometimes* ***darkness***, *but now ye are* ***light in the Lord***: *walk as* ***children of*** *light."* Satan uses darkness to enslave us. God uses light to set us free. As "children of light," we are God's beacon sent into a dark world. We are the counterculture.

To accept Jesus is to choose light, eternal life, and liberty. To reject Him is to embrace darkness, death, and bondage. Jesus spoke of being cast into outer darkness, where there will be weeping and gnashing of teeth (see Matt. 22:13; 8:12; 25:30). A place of gnashing of teeth and weeping is not a reference to heaven. It is a place of torment. If men refuse to come to the light, if they choose to embrace and love darkness, then eternity can be nothing for them but outer darkness.

Darkness is a place of sin and rebellion to God resulting in the ultimate sin of unbelief. That sin (unbelief) is the only sin not covered on the cross. This is the sin that the "Holy Spirit" convicts the world of. John 16:8 says, *"When he* [Holy Spirit] *is come, he will reprove the world of sin, and of righteousness, and of judgment."* Verse 9 goes on to say, *"of sin, because they believe not on me."* The only sin not covered on the cross is the rejection of the cross—unbelief! Unbelief is the darkness and blindness that leads to outer darkness. Believing in Jesus and the cross breaks that darkness.

We must accept God's love, extended in Jesus on the cross, by faith in order to be saved. We must be faithful to the light amid the darkness. The culture of darkness is one of sin, lies, deceit, falsehoods, and rejection of the truth. The counterculture must be one of God's righteousness, not man's. It must be truthful, honest, and faithful above all things to Jesus— the true Light of this world. John declares in 1 John 1:5-7:

*God is light and in Him is no darkness at all. If we
say that we have fellowship with Him, and walk in
darkness, we lie and do not practice the truth. But
if we walk in the light as He is in the light, we have
fellowship with one another, and the blood of Jesus
Christ His Son cleanses us from all sin.*

As children of light, we are to now walk in truth. God's
Word is truth (see John 17:17), and we now believe God's
Word above all. Revelation of God and His righteousness is
light. Understanding of His will and holiness is light. Walking
in this light is applying it to our everyday lives.

In 3 John 1:4, John declares he has *"no greater joy than to
hear that my children walk in the truth."* When we walk in the
light of God's Word (truth) it pleases God. When our faith
(what we believe) affects our actions (how we behave) it
pleases God. Faith without works (action) is dead (see James
2:17,20,22,26). Believing and behaving in accordance with
God's Word is walking in the light. Unbelief and actions contrary to God's Word is darkness.

*Thy word is a lamp unto my feet, and a light unto
my path. I have sworn, and I will perform it, that I
will keep thy righteous judgments.*

PSALM 119:105

You can see today how men love darkness and hate the
light because their deeds are evil. Evil only survives and
thrives in the darkness. Light not only exposes darkness but
expels it and overcomes it. God is calling the church to be
"the light of the world" and *"a city that is set on a hill"* (see
Matt. 5:14). To be the "light of the world" for our generation,

we must repent as God's people and walk in the light. God's Word is final authority, truth, and light in our lives.

> *For everyone practicing evil hates the light and does not come to the light, lest his deeds should be exposed. But he who does the truth comes to the light, that his deeds may be clearly seen, that they have been done in God.*
>
> JOHN 3:20

Notice the connection between light and truth:

> *Then Jesus spoke to them again, saying, "I am the light of the world. He who follows Me shall not walk in darkness, but have the light of life."*
>
> JOHN 8:12

Yes, we all fall short of the glory of God at times. We fall, fail, or stumble. However, no one born again "practices evil." As a counterculture of light, we need to be quick to repent (change our minds and direction) when falling or failing. None of us are perfect after the flesh, but all of us in the counterculture are righteous and truly holy after our spirit. Because we are now made righteous by faith, we need to always pursue doing the right things.

Paul and Barnabas were sent by God to be *"a light to the Gentiles"* (Acts 13:47). Paul spoke often of his encounter with Jesus being this overwhelming, unapproachable light (see 1 Tim. 6:16; Acts 9:3-4). Jesus is Light and in Him is no darkness at all. In Revelation we read: *"And the city had not need of the sun, neither of the moon, to shine in it: for the glory of God did* *lighten it, and **the Lamb is the light thereof***" (Rev. 21:23). Now, through our union with Christ, we are the light of this world.

This is our mission as the church in the earth today. We are preaching the same gospel and the same Jesus that Paul preached. Through the anointing of the Holy Spirit, we are commissioned by God to point our generation from darkness to light and from Satan to God so they may be saved.

> *The night is far spent, the day is at hand. Therefore let us cast off the works of darkness, and let us put on the armor of light.*
>
> ROMANS 13:12

> *For you were once darkness, but now you are light in the Lord. Walk as children of light.*
>
> EPHESIANS 5:8

Before faith in Christ, we were part of the darkness of this world. Now therefore, as children of light, we are merciful to anyone bound by darkness.

> *Do all things without complaining and disputing, that you may become blameless and harmless, children of God without fault in the midst of a crooked and perverse generation, among whom you shine as lights in the world, holding fast the word of life, so that I may rejoice in the day of Christ that I have not run in vain or labored in vain.*
>
> PHILIPPIANS 2:14-16

Because of who we are in Christ, Paul goes on to say:

Therefore let us not sleep, as others do, but let us watch and be sober. For those who sleep, sleep at night, and those who get drunk are drunk at night. But let us who are of the day be sober, putting on the breastplate of faith and love, and as a helmet the hope of salvation.

1 THESSALONIANS 5:6-8

Our heavenly Father is the Father of lights (see James 1:17), and as His children we are to be light in a dark world. God's Word is a lamp unto our feet, a light unto our path. It always shines in any dark place as we walk by faith (see 2 Pet. 1:19).

How do we know we are children of light and not of darkness? John makes it clear for all to see:

Again, a new commandment I write to you, which thing is true in Him and in you, because the darkness is passing away, and the true light is already shining. He who says he is in the light, and hates his brother, is in darkness until now. He who loves his brother abides in the light, and there is no cause for stumbling in him. But he who hates his brother is in darkness and walks in darkness, and does not know where he is going, because the darkness has blinded his eyes.

1 JOHN 2:8-11

Love is the counterculture to hate. If we are children of light, and by our new nature in Christ walking in that light, there is no place for hate. Love, which works no ill toward my neighbor, is how I know I have been delivered from the powers of darkness and translated into the Kingdom of God's dear Son.

To point out evil deeds of our culture is not mean-spirited or hate speech. Bringing attention to sin in our world is not condemning those who are bound by sin. Those living in and dying in their sins is their condemnation. God has given everyone free will to choose between light and darkness. As the counterculture, we must shine God's light into the world warning everyone of His final judgment and delivering us all from Satan to God. We must lovingly and peacefully push back on all the darkness in our world. We must speak truth in love and give people a chance to accept or reject truth for themselves. When we do not speak up, we are rejecting the truth for them.

CHAPTER 8

ARMOR OF LIGHT

The night is far spent, the day is at hand. Therefore let us cast off the works of darkness, and let us put on the armor of light.
—ROMANS 13:12

As children of light, it is our desire for everyone to experience the marvelous light and all the blessings and prosperity associated with the light of the gospel. In church culture, we are to behave in a way that exposes darkness while compelling people to come to the light. But how do we protect ourselves in a culture so different from ours and be able to stand and fight? We do it by putting on the whole armor of God (see Eph. 6:10-18).

Remember, we are in a spiritual battle with *"rulers of the darkness of this age"* (Eph. 6:12). We are not wrestling with people; demonic forces are wrestling with us.

> *For though we walk in the flesh, we do not war according to the flesh. For the weapons of our warfare are not carnal but mighty in God for pulling down strongholds.*
> 2 CORINTHIANS 10:3-4

Reproving of the works of darkness is not about harming one another. Anytime we speak out against sin, it should only be done with the heart to bring freedom to the captives of darkness. Simply put, we are in a battle *against* darkness, *for* the heart of every individual. That is why we need the armor of God. It is not a Kingdom costume we dress up in for our daily devotions then discard. It is meant to empower us to *"fight the good fight of faith"* (see 1 Tim. 6:12) and prevail against the enemy.

God's armor equips us to "war a good warfare." It enables us to stand, overcome, and prevail. It reveals our spiritual weapons that are not carnal. While Satan has an armor of darkness, God has one of light. God's armor exposes, disarms, and destroys Satan's spiritual strongholds.

> *Finally, my brethren, be strong in the Lord and in the power of His might.*
> EPHESIANS 6:10

Our offensive position in warfare is to remember that our strength is in the Lord and not ourselves. Though it is walked out in the physical realm, it is a spiritual battle. It will never be won in human ability, wisdom, or strength.

GOD'S ARMOR

Put on the whole armor of God, that you may be able to stand against the wiles of the devil.

EPHESIANS 6:11

God's armor brings His ability to every fight. The "wiles of the devil" are strategies and tactics that are weapons of darkness. The enemy has been around a long time and has a lot of experience in this spiritual battle. While he is not, and will never be, more strategic than God, he is often more strategic than us. That is why Paul says to put on the *whole* armor of God. By doing so, we can take advantage of *all* of God's power and might without leaving any exposed areas of weakness.

For we do not wrestle against flesh and blood, but against principalities, against powers, against the rulers of the darkness of this age, against spiritual hosts of wickedness in the heavenly places.

EPHESIANS 6:12

I know I've reminded you of this scripture many times, but that's because it bears repeating over and over. Ephesians 6:12 affirms who this battle is with and against. God works through people and so does Satan. So much of the battle is staying focused on who is the real enemy—Satan, not people! Fighting with people is just a distraction designed to keep us busy while Satan continues to carry out his plot against us.

When someone hurts or offends us, we must never forget that before Jesus came into our lives:

You once walked according to the course of this world, according to the prince of the power of the air, the spirit who now works in the sons of disobedience, among whom also we all once conducted ourselves.

EPHESIANS 2:3

Before Jesus we were bound by darkness, being used by Satan, and ignorant of our fallen condition. Remembering these times of pain can help us be merciful to those who have hurt us out of their own bondage and pain.

But I say to you, love your enemies, bless those who curse you, do good to those who hate you, and pray for those who spitefully use you and persecute you.

MATTHEW 5:44

The light of Jesus reveals how direct conflict with people has a negative impact in our lives, teaching us how compassion and prayer for those who would harm us exposes the real enemy—Satan.

For every piece of armor that God has, Satan has his own counterfeit. You will know which piece you're putting on by the fruit it bears in your own life. To make things easy for you, I have put together a table that compares and contrasts them side by side.

ARMOR OF LIGHT	VS	ARMOR OF DARKNESS
Truth (girdle)		Lies/deception
Righteousness (breastplate)		Guilt/condemnation/slander
Gospel of peace (feet shod)		False peace/strife/division
Faith (shield)		Unbelief (fiery darts)/fear
Salvation (helmet) — hope/ promises — mind of Christ		Oppression (helmet) — worry/ anxiety/problems — negative thoughts
Word of God (sword) — divides good and evil — life		Word of Satan (world) — divides people from God — death

GOD'S DEFENSE

Now that we understand the importance of the armor of God, let's look at the entire Scripture in Ephesians 6:13-17 and then break it down by each specific piece.

> *Therefore take up the whole armor of God, that you may be able to withstand in the evil day, and having done all, to stand. Stand therefore, having girded your waist with truth, having put on the breastplate of righteousness, and having shod your feet with the preparation of the gospel of peace; above all, taking the shield of faith with which you will be able to quench all the fiery darts of the wicked one. And take the helmet of salvation, and the sword of the Spirit, which is the word of God.*

The Girdle of Truth

> *Stand therefore, having girded your waist with truth...*
>
> EPHESIANS 6:14

Satan's strategy is to lie and deceive—about everything. Therefore, truth is our offensive weapon against darkness. Truth is what sanctifies and sets us apart from the world (see John 17:17). It is not our holiness, self-righteousness, or being *woke*; it is the power of God's Word—truth.

In John 8:31-32, Jesus was speaking to Jews who believed in Him: *"If ye continue in my word, then are ye my disciples indeed; and ye shall know the truth, and the truth shall make you free."* Truth based on God's Word and principles can bring freedom. While truth alone will not free us, knowing it will. Putting on truth as a girdle breaks the dark lies and deception of Satan.

When spoken in love, it brings maturity to us as believers (see Eph. 4:15). There is no substitute for truth, no force of nature as powerful, and no demon in hell that can prevail

WE ARE "GROUND ZERO" FOR THE TRUTH.

against it. We push back darkness by putting on truth. We are to put it on, not demand that others do so. In Matthew 4 Jesus teaches us how to fight against Satan. In all of the temptations thrown at Him, His response was, "It is written" (Matthew 4:4, 4:7, 4:10).

As a culture of light, the church is to be a refuge for the truth. In 1 Timothy 3:15, Paul speaks of how we are to behave as a part of God's family: *"I write so that you may know how you ought to conduct yourself in the house of God, which is the church of the living God, the pillar and ground of the truth."* We are "ground zero" for the truth. Without this pillar things collapse.

The church is built on the foundation of truth and will lead the way from darkness to light. According to Romans 1:18, Paul says that *"the wrath of God is revealed from heaven against all ungodliness and unrighteousness of men, who hold the truth in unrighteousness."* The New King James Version says, *"who suppress the truth in unrighteousness."* He is not talking about people falling short of the things of God, but rather people who rejected God and the truth. Hello, cancel culture!

We who have been made righteous by faith in Jesus and the cross must "proclaim the truth in love" and "practice the truth in faith." In Romans 13:14, Scripture encourages us to *"put on the Lord Jesus Christ, and make no provision for the flesh, to fulfill its lust."* When we put on Jesus, we put on truth. He is the *"way, the truth, and the life"* (John 14:6). When we proclaim and embrace truth, we embrace Jesus.

The Breastplate of Righteousness

Having put on the breastplate of righteousness...

EPHESIANS 6:14

God's righteousness of the heart and, from there, action in our life is an offensive weapon against Satan's strategies of guilt, condemnation, accusation, and offense. One of the enemy's titles is *"accuser of our brethren"* (Rev. 12:10).

He slanders God consistently. He condemns and tries to shame us into silence. By the work of the cross, God has made us righteous and free from all forms of guilt, shame, and condemnation.

> *There is therefore now no condemnation to those who are in Christ Jesus, who do not walk according to the flesh, but according to the Spirit.*
>
> ROMANS 8:1

After the flesh we are all weak and fall short of God's glory. But after the Spirit, or who we are in Christ, we can stand against the accusations of the devil. Proverbs 28:1 declares, *"the righteous are bold as a lion."* We can be bold when we have confidence in the fact that Christ has made us righteous.

> *For God made Christ, who never sinned, to be the offering for our sin, so that we could be made right with God through Christ.*
>
> 2 CORINTHIANS 5:21 (NLT)

Jesus never sinned. Instead, He took our sins upon Himself on the cross. God made Jesus sin with our sin without Him sinning. Why? So, we could be made righteous with His righteousness without works. Jesus was made sin on our behalf; therefore, we are made righteous on His.

> *For as by one man's [Adam's] disobedience many were made sinners, so also by one Man's [Jesus'] obedience many will be made righteous.*
>
> ROMANS 5:19

It is crucial that we understand this concept because it affects how we engage in warfare with the enemy. If we understand that we are righteous in Christ, when the enemy comes against us, we won't allow his schemes to defeat us.

"No weapon formed against you shall prosper, and every tongue which rises against you in judgment you shall condemn. This is the heritage of the servants of the Lord, and their righteousness is from Me," says the Lord.

ISAIAH 54:17

More often than not, the weapons of Satan's warfare are words to discourage, dismay, and disrupt our battle plans. If he can get us to believe that we are "just a poor sinner saved by grace," he won't have to do much else to keep us from realizing our true nature—the very righteousness of God in Christ. Have you ever heard these words? "Who are you to speak out? You're not perfect." This is where humility and faith work together. We are not perfect after the flesh, but only in Christ and after the Spirit are we righteous. God has forgiven us and reconciled us to Himself; will you be reconciled also? Isaiah said our righteousness is from God, not our flesh or self.

Satan will always use accusations to silence us or get us to disengage in the battle. Words like *racist, privilege*, and *homophobe* are weapons against us to try and make us back up, back down, and back out of the battle. The enemy will shame us, guilt us, and/or condemn us to push forward his agenda of hate, death, and darkness. Our message is on

Christ's behalf, not self-righteousness. His righteousness is a gift to us; will you now receive it?

When we understand how God sees us, Satan will form his weapons, but they will not prosper. When people condemn us, we can take our authority, condemn the lies, and watch God move on our behalf.

Shoes of the Gospel of Peace

> *And having shod your feet with the preparation of the gospel of peace...*
>
> EPHESIANS 6:15

The *gospel* of peace is another offensive weapon. This kind of peace is different from the world's. Because of what Christ has done on the cross, we all have the opportunity to be at peace with God. Because we are at peace with God, we can be at peace with all men. It is the gospel of peace, not just peace.

> *If it is possible, as much as depends on you, live peaceably with all men.*
>
> ROMANS 12:18

Unfortunately, not all men will choose to be at peace with God or with you. They subscribe to the world's kind of peace—a peace that promotes compromise and surrender to its culture. The world's peace desires to conform us into an image other than Christ. While that kind of peace preaches love and unity, it actually requires the surrender of morals and virtues, which requires the removal of our girdle of truth and breastplate of righteousness. If we want to have peace with the world, we must silence God. When God's Word and truth go silent, people are pulled into the pit—the pit of darkness.

> *To You I will cry, O Lord my Rock: do not be silent to*
> *me, lest, if You are silent to me, I become like those*
> *who go down to the pit.*
> PSALM 28:1

The devil wants unilateral disarmament from God's people so he can promote evil. If we let God's Word be silenced, Satan will fill that void with false peace, unity, and security to draw unsuspecting, naïve people into darkness.

> *Do not take me away with the wicked and with the*
> *workers of iniquity, who speak peace to their neigh-*
> *bors, but evil is in their hearts.*
> PSALM 28:3

They falsely promise peace while planning evil for our lives. The world's peace demands a complete denouncing of God's Word, character, and nature. If not, there will be no peace. A peace that compromises God's righteousness and holiness is one of destruction. Don't misunderstand me— we are a people of peace and should be peacemakers (see Matt. 5:9).

Our goal should always be to seek peaceful resolutions to all our social challenges of today. America's Constitution itself paves the way for peaceful protest when we see community injustice. Our form of government, derived from God's moral law, calls for civil and peaceful discourse to provide solutions to real problems that a "world in darkness" faces. Peace with God and our neighbors is one of the virtues that comes from the Kingdom of God to our hearts.

> And he shall judge among the nations, and shall rebuke many people: and they shall beat their swords into plowshares, and their spears into pruninghooks: nation shall not lift up sword against nation, neither shall they learn war any more.
>
> ISAIAH 2:4

Except for national and personal defense, we are to be at peace with all men. It is paramount to understand the difference between God's peace and the world's so-called peace. The violence (and promise of more) we see today is not a godly thing. We must not lay down our spiritual weapons in a time when disagreements and differences are escalating to the violent actions we see being played out before our eyes.

So many have disengaged from spiritual warfare in the "interest of peace." In the name of having peace with darkness, many are allowing the church to be defiled by worldly philosophies rather than standing for godly truth. Our nation is collapsing under the guise of the world's type of peace and unity. This must be rejected.

If we want to walk in true peace, we must get God's viewpoint on the subject. The most important thing for us to know is that God is at peace with us and wills nothing but good for us.

> Glory to God in the highest, and on earth peace, goodwill toward men!
>
> LUKE 2:14

These are the words declared and sung in heaven at the arrival of Jesus on earth—the good news (gospel) of who Jesus is and what He would do to save us from our sins. God loves us and has made peace with us by the blood of His cross. We need to accept that love and be at peace with Him.

Too many good Christian people think that God is warring with them. Some seem to be warring with Him. I promise you that He is not angry with us, so don't be angry with Him, ever. God has made peace through the cross and will never be at war with us. He is the source of nothing but good and goodwill toward us.

> [Jesus said,] *"Do not think that I came to bring peace on earth. I did not come to bring peace but a sword."*
> MATTHEW 10:34

Jesus' statement is a very difficult concept for many believers to process. Christ is the Prince of Peace, so why did He come to bring a sword? Remember, we are in a spiritual battle, not a physical one. It is the work of darkness that God is not at peace with.

Jesus came to expose the evil that is hiding in our world. He divides moral from immoral, light from dark, and good from evil. He revealed the glory of God so the chains binding us could be broken and we could be free.

In Romans 16:19-20 Paul is encouraging us to be *"wise in what is good, and simple concerning evil. And the God of* peace *will* **crush** *Satan under your feet shortly."* God's wisdom is required regarding good. We are to keep it simple concerning evil. If God says that something is evil, then it is and belongs under our feet as we stand! If we stand in the light, then darkness is under our feet. The God of peace doesn't compromise with Satan but rather crushes him under our feet.

Hang in there, we are halfway dressed!

The Shield of Faith

> *Above all, taking the shield of faith with which you will be able to quench all the fiery darts of the wicked one...*
>
> EPHESIANS 6:16

While faith is not mentioned first, it is declared to be *"above all."* Why? Because God's armor can only be received by and operated in faith. It's how we get and stay dressed.

Satan holds the world in darkness through unbelief. He uses doubt and fear to cause us to waver, rendering us ineffective in our battles. Faith is how we please God and overcome the world (see Heb. 11:6; 1 John 5:4-5). Faith is our simple trust in God and His Word. Faith is how we know that God keeps His promises. Faith believes in the love God has for us and the assurance of His goodness. In short, it is our simple response to God's amazing grace.

> *Trust in the Lord with all your heart, and lean not on your own understanding; in all your ways acknowledge Him, and He shall direct your paths. Do not be wise in your own eyes; fear the Lord and depart from evil.*
>
> PROVERBS 3:5-7

Faith simply trusts God and His goodness regardless of our circumstances or lack of understanding. When I simply cannot explain what I'm facing, I choose to look to God and trust Him.

> *You will keep him in perfect peace, whose mind is stayed on You, because he trusts in You. Trust in the Lord forever, for in YAH, the Lord, is everlasting strength.*
>
> ISAIAH 26:3-4

We can't trust God independent of our thoughts or mind. Setting our thoughts on Him is a part of how faith works. The shield of faith quenches all the fiery darts of doubt and unbelief. We walk and fight a good fight by faith. Faith is our response to fear and unbelief. Satan uses fear to get us to respond in unbelief to the challenges of this life. What we choose to listen to or set our minds on is going to either release faith or fear. Faith comes by hearing and listening to God's Word. His promises are sure and reliable. Getting focused on God's faithfulness and loving-kindness causes faith to rise and counter fear.

> *Therefore I remind you to stir up the gift of God which is in you through the laying on of my hands. For God has not given us a spirit of fear, but of power and of love and of a sound mind.*
>
> 2 TIMOTHY 1:6-7

Paul is reminding Timothy to not forget the gift that is in him but instead to stir it up! Any fear you face is not of God. Remember that God's love is in you and His power is available when you fix your mind on Him. The anxiety that is being cultivated through politics and the "woke" culture is being used to enslave the masses. This must be resisted by faith in a powerful, loving God. The fear of COVID-19 is much more dangerous than the virus. God is not the author of all this fear; it must be resisted by faith in God's promises.

The Helmet of Salvation

And take the helmet of salvation...
EPHESIANS 6:17

In the Greek, the word for *salvation* is *soteria*, which means "rescue or safety (physically or morally), deliver, health, save, saving" (Strong's G4991). Putting on the helmet of salvation in Jesus protects our minds from Satan's thoughts of lack, worry, and fear. In our battle with darkness, distraction is Satan's goal. We cannot win against distraction if our minds are not set on God's salvation. Like a helmet, our thoughts must be set on the promises of God, rather than the problems of this life. It is the mind of Christ that gives us hope in all the challenges of our world. This is how we guard our hearts, affecting in a positive way, the issues of our lives (see Prov. 4:23). The battlefield of the mind is where the warfare is won in the early stage of every fight.

Focusing our thoughts on Jesus releases power to overcome darkness. I'm not saying our power comes from the mind, but it does come through it. Setting our minds on Jesus and His word empowers us to be spiritually minded, thereby producing life and peace. Much of our spiritual battle takes place in the field of our minds.

For to be carnally minded is death, but to be spiritually minded is life and peace.
ROMANS 8:6

I'm not saying all our problems are "just in our heads," but rather how we perceive and process them can either release fear and death or life and peace. When our thoughts drift to the storms and challenges of this life, our faith can shipwreck. Unfortunately, many people's faith has shipwrecked because they do not use the helmet of salvation to protect themselves from philosophies of this world (see Col. 2:8).

> *If then you were raised with Christ, seek those things which are above, where Christ is, sitting at the right hand of God. Set your mind on things above, not on things on the earth. For you died, and your life is hidden with Christ in God. When Christ who is our life appears, then you also will appear with Him in glory.*
>
> COLOSSIANS 3:1-4

We "seek those things above" by setting our thoughts and emotions "on things above, not on things on the earth." We are to feast our thoughts on all the heavenly treasures and realities we now have in Jesus. When we allow our thoughts to go contrary to Jesus and His Word, we become ineffective in warfare.

The Sword of the Spirit

> *And the sword of the Spirit, which is the word of God.*
>
> EPHESIANS 6:17

Last, but certainly not least, our final weapon is the sword of the Spirit. When we speak, sing, or pray the heartfelt Word of God in faith, we're wielding a powerful spiritual weapon that cuts Satan's influence to the core, forcing him to retreat in torment, fully exposed as the father of lies.

> *For the word of God is living and powerful, and sharper than any two-edged sword, piercing even to the division of soul and spirit, and of joints and marrow, and is a discerner of the thoughts and intents of the heart.*
>
> HEBREWS 4:12

When Scripture speaks of the heart, it is referring to the combination of our soul and spirit. The true intentions of our hearts are the hardest things in the universe to divide or discern. God's Word is the only thing that can do both. In addition to our hearts, the sword of the Spirit divides and discerns light from dark, good from evil, sheep from goats, just to mention a few. Jesus is described in Revelation 1:16 as having:

> *In His right hand seven stars, out of His mouth went a sharp two-edged sword, and His countenance was like the sun shining in its strength.*

Jesus creates, chastens, and judges with the words of His mouth. Everything was created by His Word: *"And God said"* (Gen. 1:3). Hebrews 1:3 teaches us that He upholds *"all things by the word of His power."* Everything responds to His word, including Satan.

> *And to the angel of the church in Pergamos write, "These things says He who has the sharp two-edged sword: 'I know your works, and where you dwell, where Satan's throne is. And you hold fast to My*

name, and did not deny My faith even in the days in which Antipas was My faithful martyr, who was killed among you, where Satan dwells."

REVELATION 2:12-13

Jesus goes on to correct them with issues concerning the doctrine of Balaam and the doctrine of the Nicolaitans, which He hates. In verse 16 He says, *"Repent, or else I will come to you quickly and will **fight** against them with the **sword of My mouth**."*

The church of the Laodiceans was corrected for their lukewarmness: *"As many as I love, I rebuke and chasten. Therefore be zealous and repent"* (Rev. 3:19). God's Word is a sword. It purges, corrects, chastens, and, if need be, brings judgment to Satan's works. He uses His words to fight darkness, so why shouldn't we? In Matthew 4 Jesus teaches us how to fight against Satan. In all of the temptations through at Him, His response was, *"It is written"* (Matt. 4:4, 4:7, 4:10).

God's Word spoken out of a heart of faith is miraculous. It works immediately in the spiritual realm and, in time, affects the natural. Paul encourages a young pastor Timothy on how to fight a good fight and skillfully battle darkness:

> *Timothy, my son, here are my instructions for you, based on the prophetic words spoken about you earlier. May they help you fight well in the Lord's battles.*
>
> 1 TIMOTHY 1:18 (NLT)

God's Word spoken over us enables us to war a good warfare. God's Word spoken to our mountains causes them to be removed (see Mark 11:23-24). Read the Word, meditate on the Word, then speak it, sing it, and pray it! All six pieces of God's armor are the armor of light that can fight against evil. This armor is what equips us to be the counterculture to hate, death, and darkness. So get dressed, stay dressed, and fight the good fight of faith! Don't charge hell in the buff with only a water pistol! There are far too many Christian streakers fighting a losing battle. We can only be effective as a counterculture by being dressed in God's armor of light.

CHAPTER 9

RACISM

Having, reflecting, or fostering the belief
that race is a fundamental determinant of
human traits and capacities and that racial
differences produce an inherent superiority
of a particular race; of, relating to, or
characterized by the systemic oppression
of a racial group to the social, economic,
and political advantage of another.
—MERRIAM-WEBSTER

Baptist minister and leader of the American civil rights movement Martin Luther King, Jr. said in 1963, "I have a dream that my four little children will one day live in a nation where they will not be judged by the color of their skin but by the content of their character."

Every believer in Jesus carries that same dream in their heart. We don't hear Dr. King's peaceful protest speeches or even his dream quoted much anymore. The culture of hate, death, and darkness judges everything and everyone based on color.

To even suggest someone is wrong or their actions are unacceptable is considered oppressive, and in some circles deemed racist. Character, or the lack thereof, doesn't seem to matter anymore in many parts of our country, and in some cases color is all that still matters.

In Chapter 3 I briefly touched on racism regarding the culture of hate. I firmly believe that a subject as misunderstood and important as this one requires more attention. Many in our culture and government would have us believe that racism is dominating our country. They say that not only is it prevalent in white culture, but it is, in fact, part of the systems that operate our country. They call it "systemic racism." It is being conveyed as truth that white people, specifically white men, are purposely and methodically oppressing anyone of color, especially black people. As if that weren't bad enough, some are trying to get young people to believe that if they were born white, they are born racist. That is absolutely false.

Racism is a sin of the heart and cannot find any similitude of refuge in the church. Like all sin, it destroys lives and poisons the mind. My father taught me that racism is taught— no one is born a racist. To suggest someone is a racist based on the color of their skin *is* racism. There should be no tolerance for evil no matter how loud the world demands it.

Racism is one of many evils that plague the human heart and must be opposed.

> *Let love be without dissimulation. Abhor that which is evil; cleave to that which is good.*
>
> ROMANS 12:9

Dissimulation in the Greek is *anapokritos* and means "hypocrisy" (Strong's G505). We are being hypocrites when we don't stand up against all forms of racism. God's love is to abhor evil while clinging to good. Love, God's kind, does not embrace and celebrate any form of evil. The culture says it's love to accept, embrace, and celebrate what God calls evil. We cannot be hypocritical in our love. Sin must be opposed regardless of the heart it abides and hides in. Anyone of any color can be a racist. Many accusing others of racism are guilty of it in their own hearts.

> *When you say they are wicked and should be punished, you are condemning yourself, for you who judge others do these very same things.*
>
> ROMANS 2:1 (NLT)

Sigmund Freud called this "psychological projection." Many are projecting onto others the sins of their own hearts. Regardless of political ideology, this is a common tactic used by corrupt officials. They accuse innocent people of the very things they are guilty of, putting the guiltless on the defense while distracting from and covering up their own crimes. For prime examples, accusing others of "Russian collusion" while they are actually colluding with the Russians, and accusing a sitting president of being illegitimate while they plan to steal an upcoming election. The reason many won't point out these things or expose them is for fear they will be accused of being a GOP, right-wing fanatic, racist, or domestic terrorist. When God calls on us, we can't fear people because that can become a snare (see Prov. 29:25).

WEAPONIZED RACISM

Racism is being weaponized to silence any opposition to evil. Any opposition to any form of hate, death, or darkness is labeled racism. People have tried to define and redefine who is a racist and what racism is. For example, in today's culture, anyone who opposes the far left's agenda is called a racist. Conservatives are accused of being racist for their moral and traditional values. Support for law enforcement is considered racism. If you believe violence and looting is wrong, it's because you're a racist. This is all so wrong and cannot be a part of the counterculture. All these false accusations are by design. The culture of hate knows how to use evil accusations of racism to silence people because no one wants to be thought of as a racist.

So, what is racism? As defined at the start of this chapter, it is "a belief that race is the *primary determinant of human traits and capacities* and that racial differences produce an inherent superiority of a particular race." Simply put, racism is when a person or a group of people are known and judged by the color of their skin instead of their character, accomplishments, personality, or contribution to society.

So to be a racist, or for a system to be racist, there must be an obsession with skin color. In a society or culture where sin abounds, racism will be one of many sins. God's grace is the answer to all sin. Romans 5:20 says, *"where sin abounded, grace did much more abound.*" All abounding sin, including racism, is defeated in God's amazing grace.

The sin of racism in our world today is not coming from a single source or group alone. For example, in politics right now, many people are not put in authority based on their qualifications, wisdom, fear of the Lord, character, or virtue. Rather, news outlets excitedly report "the first woman ever appointed," "the first person of color to," and "the first gay or transgender." Taking an objective look at this language, it's easy to see that politics has become more about identity than good policy or capacity to lead. People are celebrated based on gender or color, not qualifications. Others are falsely judged based solely on color.

A person, especially an elected official, should be judged by their character and their deeds instead of their gender, skin color, or sexual orientation. Solomon said it best in Proverbs 20:11: *"Even small children are known by their actions"* (NIV). We are to be known and judged by our actions, not the color of our skin.

Jesus says in John 7:24, *"Do not judge according to appearance, but judge with righteous judgment."* Everything and everyone is being judged by their outer appearance. However, when we judge with righteous judgments, we are accosted. We must stop judging by appearance and make righteous judgments according to Jesus. To say that *all* white people are…(you fill in the blank) or that *all* black people are…(you fill in the blank) is racism.

Most children do not see each other by race unless taught to do so. They choose who to play with based on whether the child is kind, helpful, funny—those type of characteristics. If taught to love God, love their neighbor as themselves, and the "Golden Rule"—Do unto others as you would have them do unto you—they mature as adults with no racism in their hearts. This is known in God's Kingdom as "Critical *Grace* Theory." God's grace teaches respect and value of all human life. Honor and respect for your fellow man knows no color. "Critical *Grace* Theory" promotes forgiveness and reconciliation with God and each other. It declares the gospel as God's power of salvation. The preaching of the cross is God's power to change our hearts and thereby society at large. Scriptures teach it is sin that separates us from God and one another. It is God's grace that brings us into fellowship with God and one another.

Along with racism comes the term "white privilege," which has become a platform to further divide people based on skin color. According to those who believe in this tool of division, "white privilege" is the idea that all white people have an easier time in life simply because they are white. Recently, this platform has denied many white people a voice in social and political matters. Some believe that Caucasians don't understand anything else other than their "whiteness." Again, this is completely false and racist.

To suggest that a black person has knowledge that a white person doesn't or can't have (or vice versa) is racist. It declares that one's race is superior to another or that the color of someone's skin determines superiority or inferiority. Just as poverty, crime, injustice, and addiction is not exclusive to skin color, privilege is not either. I've personally been told that I can't understand certain issues because I am white. God's Word is where all of us should gain understanding of right and wrong, not worldly knowledge, especially when based on the color of one's skin or ethnic culture. Experiential knowledge does not make one superior or others inferior. Revelation knowledge from God's Word and Holy Spirit teaches us good and evil, right from wrong, independent of our human experiences. I don't have to have an affair to understand the evil or pain of adultery. I don't have to have cancer to hate it or help people experiencing it.

PRIVILEGE

I will acknowledge that there is a lot of privilege in our world today. Personally, I went to school with a star athlete who skipped classes and still graduated with honors. Athletic privilege is everywhere. Hollywood privilege is as well. Their opinions and voices on matters seem to get heard often and carry more weight than us underlings. They get special attention and favors just because of their "star" status, no matter what their skin color is. While this may not be true of all athletes or Hollywood stars, my point is that there is privilege all around us and no one seems to acknowledge it as such or call it out unless their opinions align with God's righteousness and Kingdom principles.

Liberal privilege allows one to commit horrible crimes and get a pass in the media and, in some cases, even promotions. Big Tech privilege allows them to manipulate elections and censor anyone who does not go along with their chosen narrative. They've created the cancel culture that determines what is truth and what are lies. Bureaucrats can break the law with impunity—political privilege. Only in God and the light of the gospel will we experience mutual respect, value, and equality among all people.

It's unfortunate that illegal aliens can enter our country and receive money, health care, education, and other benefits that are paid for by hardworking American taxpayers, while many law-abiding citizens are being denied the same resources. Those who dare speak out about this hypocrisy are labeled racist, bigots, and intolerant. Their words are deemed hate speech and they are persecuted and mocked.

FIGHTING RACISM WITH RACISM, EVEN PERCEIVED RACISM, WILL NEVER WORK.

Even though I know that I am writing this with love in my heart toward all people, it seems inevitable that I will be called insensitive, uncaring, and guilty of sounding negative and accusatory. It appears obvious that all of us will be falsely accused unless we agree with the culture of hate, death, and darkness.

The Oxford Dictionary says that "racism is the belief that certain races are better than others; *discrimination against* or *hostile toward* those of *other races*." It doesn't get much more straightforward than that. When we are hostile toward people of another color, that's racism. No matter the color of someone's skin, if the beliefs of their heart fall within this definition, they are racists and need to repent and ask for forgiveness and receive healing.

Don't misunderstand me—I am not naïve to the fact that there are racist white people around the world. But to say that every member of any people group practices the same sin is racism itself. Fighting racism with racism, even perceived racism, will never work. We must wake up to this lie and understand that it is manipulation by those who seek to destroy our country. They know that if they can get us busy fighting each other, we won't see them carry out their plan of destruction. Are there white racists? Absolutely. Are all white people racists? Absolutely not.

While the current culture makes everything about race, the counterculture is one of grace. We must not allow the culture to define us after color, gender, or identity politics. We are all made one in Jesus. Being male or female, Jew or Gentile, black or white, rich or poor is not where we find our identity.

> *So in Christ Jesus you are all children of God through faith, for all of you who were baptized into Christ have clothed yourselves with Christ. There is neither Jew nor Gentile, neither slave nor free, nor is there male and female, for you are all one in Christ Jesus.*
> GALATIANS 3:26-28 (NIV)

The counterculture is one of identity with Christ. Because He empowers us to do all things, it is from Him that we derive our strength (see Phil. 4:13). No matter the color of our skin, it is not privilege that prospers us. It is God who gives us that gift (see Deut. 8:18). As the spiritual seed of Abraham, we are a blessed people and should never apologize for that. Regardless of skin color, we are seated in heavenly places and declared victors, not victims, in Christ.

EQUALLY LOVED BY GOD

For those who have been judged by their skin color, it's important for you to know that the horrible sin of racism is not one the American majority condones. Most people of faith do not evaluate people by the color of their skin. Like all sin, racism should be opposed everywhere we find it.

We are equally loved and provided for in God's amazing grace. We are equal before God in value, worth, and accountability. While we are all equal, we are not the same. We all have different strengths, weaknesses, gifts, and callings. Our differences match our divine design for a divine purpose. They need to be celebrated, not used to divide us.

As the counterculture, we must understand Christ's view of equality:

> *Therefore, from now on, we regard no one according to the flesh. Even though we have known Christ according to the flesh, yet now we know Him thus no longer. Therefore, if anyone is in Christ, he is a new creation; old things have passed away; behold all things have become new.*
>
> 2 CORINTHIANS 5:16-17

In a culture where people are defined by politics, race, sexual orientation, and social class, we must respond by understanding that our identity in Christ makes us one in Him. We are given equal access to God and His throne, equal authority in His Name, and the same Holy Spirit, armor, and inheritance. If we truly want to be the counterculture in this world, we must consistently strive to live out biblical concepts and defend them in our nation.

> *So, from now on, we refuse to evaluate people merely by their outward appearances. For that's how we*

once viewed the Anointed One, but no longer do we see him with limited human insight.

2 C<small>ORINTHIANS</small> 5:16 (TPT)

CHAPTER 10

MARXISM

Karl Marx (1818-1883) was a German philosopher, econ-
omist, sociologist, and revolutionary socialist. Being a
descendant from a long line of rabbis, Marx was born
to Jewish parents in 1818. In an effort to gain influence, his father converted his family to Lutheranism.
While Marx grew up in church, he later became an
atheist. The bulk of his secondary education came
from the University of Berlin where he studied law
and philosophy. After graduating, he became the
editor for the liberal newspaper *Rheinische Zeitung*.
Due to the nature of his beliefs expressed through
his writings, he was eventually expelled from Prus-
sia, Belgium, and France.

Despite being denied British citizenship, he set-
tled in London. It was there that he and his friend,
Friedrich Engels, began publishing several books
and articles. The most well-known is titled *The*

Communist Manifesto. Marx had trouble keeping a job and was supported by Engels. He died in relative poverty in 1883 of pleurisy. His works were mostly obscure until the rise of socialism in Europe during the late 19th and early 20th centuries, when leaders of the now defunct USSR, Vladimir Lenin and Josef Stalin, rose to power.

Today, his influence can be seen in countries including Cuba and China. It is difficult to pinpoint exactly what it means to be a modern-day Marxist, as his adherents modify his teachings according to their personal interpretations. However, Karl Marx's main focus consisted of the following five points: 1) social evolution, 2) redistribution of wealth, 3) capitalism, 4) religion, and 5) the revolution.

SOCIAL EVOLUTION

Much like Charles Darwin's Theory of Evolution, Karl Marx believed in the evolution of societies, economies, and governments and that communism would be the final evolution of social structure to have a just and moral society. As an atheist, he saw no need for God in any civilized society and taught that to be a just and equitable society we all must rely on the government for our needs. From his viewpoint, a capitalist economy with free commerce and trade was the cause of all the socioeconomical woes. On the other hand, communism was the utopia of social structures. He saw socialism as the means of transfer between the two types of economies and the pathway to evolve into communism.

Once the economy was controlled by the government, so were the people. Freedom and individual rights were a threat to the collective and had to be subservient or submissive to the government or state. If necessary, the government would reconcile all things either by socialism (by voting or through ballots) or communism (through force and bullets). The free markets and commerce of capitalism plus the freedom of conscience on who and how to worship (religion) were the problem. God brings freedom of movement, thought, and speech that cannot be tolerated under Marxism. The freedom of ideas was unacceptable as well.

Dissent was a death sentence. Marx truly believed that in order to be a just and equitable society, we must put our trust in and rely on the government for our needs and lives. Both God and capitalism must be abolished and considered enemies of the state to evolve into communism. This is why we see both under assault in our politics, media, and many of our educational institutions. We must understand that communism is not utopianism. It is an evil that must be opposed at every level. It is dystopia—a society characterized by human misery, squalor, oppression, disease, and overcrowding.

2. REDISTRIBUTION OF WEALTH

> From each according to his ability, unto each according to his need.
> —KARL MARX

What he means by this is the redistribution of wealth. He thought it was just and moral to take from the "haves" and give to the "have-nots." He justified this form of theft by saying that all the "haves" took their wealth from the poor and that the poor are poor by no fault of their own. While it may be true that some people are poor through no fault of their own (i.e., born into poverty as I was), it is not true that the wealthy have stolen their wealth in an effort to keep others down.

This "oppressors vs. oppressed" scenario (or straw man) is presented so that punishing the oppressors and rewarding the oppressed can appear just and moral. This point is always presented as having compassion and desiring equity for all. In truth, it convinces the poor that they have no power and are victims of the wealthy. It is the epitome of greed and covetousness.

3. CAPITALISM

> Capitalism is the oppressor of the masses.
>
> —KARL MARX

Like any man-made system, capitalism can be corrupted (i.e., crony capitalism, which is another book in and of itself). However, capitalism has lifted more people out of poverty than any other system in this world. It allows upward mobility for all who wish to participate. Unlike socialism that equally distributes poverty and misery, capitalism allows the freedom to be poor or prosperous. You can pursue your God-given dream and happiness. It offers the opportunity for you to see a problem and create the solution. Can it be selfish? Yes, depending on the heart. Is socialism selfish? Yes, all the time, regardless of the heart. At the core of socialism is a lust for power and control.

Socialism enslaves those who create wealth, confiscates the fruits of their labor, and redistributes it to the masses who have been taught, through decades of indoctrination, to depend on government handouts from cradle to grave.

Marx believed that, in time, capitalism would be rejected for socialism. Capitalism itself ruined the plan by elevating all who wanted to participate.

With an education, good work ethic, creativity, and freedom, one could break out of the cycle of poverty. That is the American dream and story. Workers were able to buy into a company or start their own. My personal story involved believing God and His plan for my life, which broke the poverty mindset in my life and set me free to pursue my dreams.

The resilience of capitalism delayed the demonic plan of a one world order under communist tyranny, but the slow drip process of indoctrination has taken its toll:

- No one is sinful, just oppressed.
- A victim mindset is taught to divide and conquer.
- Chaos and strife are deployed to manufacture a crisis.
- The government that creates the crisis is now the solution.

Karl Marx's philosophy concerning economic theories is what drives socialism and communism. Much of America's decline over the past 60 years is rooted in his teachings.

4. RELIGION

Religion is the opium of the masses allowing the evil of capitalism to exist.

—KARL MARX

Marxism, socialism, and communism are all atheistic philosophies and governance. They are all influenced by the spirit of the antichrist because they attempt to offer other solutions to sin and false redemption. Sin is redefined under Marxism and all injustices and inequities are reconciled by the government instead of the cross.

The idolatrous worship of the state replaces the worship of God. This is why we have seen an attempt to remove God from all public arenas and anyone of faith from government. The removal of the Ten Commandments, Bibles, and prayer from our schools was not by accident but design. Faith in God, His Word, and going to church are the biggest threats to Marxism because belief in God promotes free thinking. Marxism cannot thrive among free thinkers; therefore, God must be removed for the god of government to assume the throne.

5. THE REVOLUTION

According to Marx, the answer to social class structure, capitalism, and religion is what he calls "The Revolution." In *The Communist Manifesto*, Karl Marx describes his idea of what a revolution looks like. There were two groups of people—the proletariat (working class) and the bourgeoisie (wealthy, ruling class). The bourgeoisie were in control of manufacturing and the working class were "selling their labor power in return for wages." The working class would eventually overthrow the ruling class and establish a new government where everything is to be shared equally and everyone is considered to be the same. His writings convinced millions to follow, but history has proven countless times that communism doesn't work.

While modern-day Marxism is more ambiguous, its goal has not changed. It still desires to overthrow and dig up our capitalist, Christian roots and replace them with socialism. Whether we know it or not, the ground has already been laid and the Marxist agenda is permeating every aspect of our country. This is how it works:

For Marxism to succeed in ushering in socialism, a conflict of classes must arise. You must create and exploit "oppressors" and the "the oppressed." The oppressor class must be identified and demonized. The oppressed must be convinced that they are victims of the oppressors. The oppressors can be a small group, but the oppressed must be multiple groups with a common enemy (the oppressors). The oppressors in our culture today are said to be white, native born, heterosexual, cisgender (one who identifies with the sex or gender of one's birth), Christian males. The oppressed make up anything not on that list— blacks or other people of color (not white), women, homosexuals, lesbians, transgender, illegal immigrants, etc. But that's not all. In order for this to work, we must expand the grievance class.

This is where intersectionality comes in. Have you ever wondered what LGBTQA+ has to do with civil rights? *Oppression.* The same oppressors of the black community oppress the members of the gay community, and there you have it—intersectionality.

There are even more "links" or places where there is an intersection of the oppressed by the same oppressors. Women are a part of the oppressed group, so if you are black and a woman you are doubly oppressed. If you are black, a woman, and transgender then you sit at the head of the table of victims of the oppressors.

Once the two classes are identified, you must create chaos and division between them. They begin to fight each other and then the government steps in, punishes the oppressors, and becomes the savior and redeemer of the oppressed.

Does this sound familiar to anyone besides me? Now let me tell you how it ends:

The government eventually exploits the ones they say they're helping, causing further division and victimization until eventually they have taken full control. Before people even realize what has happened, they're under a socialist regime—a regime that is now on the fast track to full-blown communism.

GOVERNMENT ABUSE

When government replaces God, it persecutes, prosecutes, and, in time, executes all noncompliant worshipers. If you refuse to worship your appointed god, it will not fare well with you as biblical and human history record. Unaccountable kings, lords, and governments have brought much misery and human suffering into the world. The third chapter of Daniel shows what can happen to a people when its leaders are not held accountable.

The three Hebrew children, Shadrach, Meshach, and Abednego, were objects of government abuse, power, and persecution. King Nebuchadnezzar's command to worship a graven image was met with opposition by the three boys. They refused to bow down and worship the image.

The king gave them opportunity to compromise, but they would not disobey God even though the command came from the king. They feared God, not man, and it brought persecution with the threat of execution. They refused to disobey God in any command to obey man. The king was enraged when the boys refused to bow and threatened them, saying:

> But if ye worship not, ye shall be cast the same hour
> into the midst of a burning fiery furnace.
>
> DANIEL 3:15

The boys still refused, so they were bound with ropes and cast into the fire. It was so hot that the men throwing them into the furnace died from the heat. The boys were divinely protected from the fire and not even their clothes smelled of smoke. The only thing burned were the ropes used to bind them. Ultimately, the king acknowledged and even praised God because of God's power to save the boys.

Similarly, it was an abuse of power and corrupt government that threw Daniel into the lions' den. King Darius was a good king, but other officials were jealous and corrupt. Government leaders plotted against him and his faith in God. Daniel was a man of prayer, so these corrupt officials had a law passed designed to entrap him. He was also a man of principle, and they knew they could use his very faith and disciplines against him. They even deceived the king to enforce a decree that outlawed prayer to any god or man but the king.

If disobeyed, the punishment was a trip to the lions' den. Daniel violated this decree by continuing his custom of praying to the one true God three times a day. He was sentenced to death by being thrown to the lions to be eaten alive. The king eventually recognized the scheme of these officials and fasted for Daniel's deliverance. God stopped the lions' mouths from consuming Daniel. Judgment was then passed on these men and their families, and they received the same punishment that they had ordered for anyone disobeying the decree. The corruption we see in government today is nothing new. However, the real tragedy is a generation blind to this danger and having no understanding of the value of freedom.

Haman was a corrupt government leader under King Ahasuerus of Persia. He sought to eliminate the entire nation of Israel because of his hatred for Mordecai, Queen Esther's cousin. Haman built a gallows to hang Mordecai. God used Queen Esther to save the Jewish nation and Haman ended up hanging on his own gallows. While it turned out well for Shadrach, Meshach, Abednego, Daniel, Mordecai, and Esther, we must learn from biblical history never to relinquish our freedoms to further empower corrupt government.

THE COLLECTIVE

Remember that Marxism is about the group (the collective), not any individuals. Until the entire group of victims is somehow elevated, they are still victims and are to be treated differently. If you are in the oppressor group yet never prosper and live a totally defeated life, you still are labeled a person of privilege, a racist (even if you don't know it), homophobic, misogynistic pig (I added the pig!). This is the language of the oppressed. The Marxist says that government is the only solution to all these social iniquities and forms of injustice.

God simply does not think this way and America does not have to go down a dark road. Our founding documents protect us from abusive government. They restrict what government can and cannot do to us. These protections and rights are from God, not man, so man cannot take them away. However, we have a responsibility to speak up about what is happening in our government—to hold our nation's elected officials accountable for what they do and don't do. Fortunately, the counterculture to Marxism is beginning to rise among the young people. People are beginning to speak out, and "cancel culture" will not be able to silence them forever.

This counterculture is creating a movement based on truth and freedom. Simply put, the gospel is the antidote to Marxism.

It is for freedom that Christ has set us free.

GALATIANS 5:1 (NIV)

The problems we are facing in our culture are sins of the heart. Where Karl Marx operated under the spirit of antichrist and offered two groups as the problem and government as the solution, God offers two men—Adam and Jesus. One was the problem and the other is the solution. You are either lost in Adam or saved through Christ. In Adam all are made sinners and live in hate, death, and darkness. Through faith in Christ, we can be made righteous and now live in love, life, and light. At the cross, Jesus reversed what Adam did in the Garden of Eden.

In God's Kingdom, where forgiveness and mercy are available to all who ask, the poor are to be cared for, the weak given double honor, and human life treated with love and respect. In Marxism there is only hate, violence, destruction, disunity, and division. Don't be deceived, Marxism always comes with an alluring façade of "just causes" wrapped in compassion and fairness; but behind that curtain, you'll find Satan pulling the strings, posing as an "angel of light" with the sole purpose of enslaving humanity. It is only in Christ Jesus that we find the counterculture of love, peace, order, and unity of the Spirit. Marxism creates an oppressed class and promises justice to the oppressors, through reparations and punishment. The cross offers forgiveness and redemption to the oppressors *and* the oppressed.

This is why Jesus commands us to go into all the world and teach to observe all He has commanded and make disciples of all nations (see Matt. 28:18-20). People need to hear the truth of what Christ offers for those who will accept it. It is why He calls us to mind renewal (see Rom. 12:2). He understands that until we live life with His perspective, we are susceptible to lies of this world. Ultimately, He calls us to speak His Word in love with authority and power (see Acts 4:13,29,31; 8:5-6) so that the lies of the enemy can be exposed and the captives can be set free.

NOTES ON KARL MARX

https://en.wikipedia.org/wiki/Karl_Marx

https://www.investopedia.com/terms/k/karl-marx.asp

https://www.history.com/topics/germany/karl-marx

https://plato.stanford.edu/entries/marx/

https://www.britannica.com/biography/Karl-Marx

http://www.historyguide.org/intellect/marx.HTML

CHAPTER 11

CULTURAL MARXISM

At the time of this writing (2020–2021), the rise of Marxism in our culture is alarming. Until now, I have never seen it as a threat to the church or the nation because it has always been a fringe group of people with limited influence. Today it drives our politics through organizations like Black Lives Matter, Inc. (BLM) and Antifa, a so-called anti-fascist movement formed in response to right-wing extremism.

Marxism saturates our primary and secondary schooling with Critical Race Theory (CRT) and stays at the forefront of our society via Big Tech and other media intent on advancing their own agenda. Just the term itself, *cultural Marxism*, is met with suspicion and false accusations of conspiracy theory. Those saturated in it are quick to deny its very existence.

Satan's greatest lie is that he doesn't exist. Why would his messengers transforming themselves as angels of light be any different (see 2 Cor. 11:14-15)? Like leaven, Marxism has permeated the culture, passing as a solution to our nation's problems when, in fact, it *is* the problem.

Do you remember reading that it is hard to know exactly what a modern-day Marxist believes because its adherents consistently modify it to suit their perspectives and agendas? That is never truer than in American Marxism today. While Karl Marx thought that socioeconomic evolution was inevitable, his philosophy was based on a working class overthrowing the ruling one—that it would only take one grievance class to create enough strife and chaos to bring down the system.

A modern-day American Marxist adapts Marx's ideas to fit around a race narrative and multiple groups that are oppressed and considered victims. Through Critical Race Theory (CRT), they are even attempting to teach our very young that if born white they are oppressors and if born black they are oppressed.

CRT is rooted in Marxism. It uses the Marxist strategy of turning the "oppressed" against the "oppressors." It builds on the completely false racism narrative that we discussed in Chapter 9—America is a racist nation, and because its founders were flawed, racist slave owners, the Constitution is a racist document.

Today, even if they don't know it, all whites are racist, steeped in white privilege, white supremacists and oppressors victimizing black people. Not only does CRT reaffirm all of this, but it wants to teach white children to apologize for the color of their skin and black children to hate and have a prejudice toward their white friends. These concepts should be opposed by all people of conscience.

White people (the oppressors) are to live in a perpetual state of guilt and apologize for their whiteness.

> *There is therefore now no condemnation to those who are in Christ Jesus, who do not walk according to the flesh, but according to the Spirit.*
>
> ROMANS 8:1

God has set us free from all this guilt and condemnation that is being used for a political agenda. We do not walk according to our flesh (white or black) but now according to the Spirit (new creation in our spirit). Hebrews 9:14 declares that the blood of Jesus has sanctified us for the purifying of the flesh, and now:

> *How much more shall the blood of Christ, who through the eternal Spirit offered Himself without spot to God, cleanse your conscience from dead works to serve the living God.*

Faith in the cross brings God's forgiveness of all sin to every one of us and purges our conscience so we don't have to live a life in perpetual guilt and shame. Christ has set us free, and whom the Son sets free is free indeed (see John 8:36).

Cultural Marxism creates chaos, division, anger, and resentment, birthing a grievance society of oppressed victims. In the eyes of American Marxism, the only way for there to be equity and justice is for the oppressors to understand any crime committed by a non-white is simply an outcry of their oppression. Any accountability for crimes committed against society or citizens is just another form of racism.

The cultural Marxist believes that change comes from the outside. They believe they have the right to condemn and shame anyone they deem as an oppressor. If those tactics don't work, "militant Marxism" is next! Hate, violence, and riots are deployed to bring down the perceived systemic, biased, unjust, unequitable system of "white privilege," replacing it with a "Big Brother" surveillance state forcefully balancing the scales. The sad thing is history has proven socialism and communism never work. Political correctness (cultural Marxism) always leads to political tyranny (militant Marxism)—The Revolution.

A One News Now article titled "Critical Race Theory: A Bait and Switch Tactic Infiltrating the Church" reports the following:

> Critical Race Theory (often referred to as CRT) teaches that American culture is rife with white supremacy and baked in racism and is used often subconsciously—to hold women and people of color back. According to Pastor and talk show host Abraham Hamilton III, it's the philosophy behind identity politics and comes straight out of the Marxist playbook.[1]

The philosophies of Marxism and CRT are even entering the church and defiling the faith of individuals and mainstream denominations.

Their goals are not to just divide us socially, but as Christians to further diminish our power against darkness.

This is all designed to bring disagreements, disputes, and strife among us, which is something God hates. Proverbs 6:16-19 says:

> *These six things the Lord hates, yes, seven are an abomination to Him: a proud look, a lying tongue, hands that shed innocent blood, a heart that devises wicked plans, feet that are swift in running to evil, a false witness who speaks lies, and one who sows discord among brethren.*

These are seven deadly and destructive sins. They are destructive to individuals and society at large. God hates them, so as believers, we should also.

How can this be? Take a moment and think about how anti-gospel this theory is. It does not address personal sin, responsibility and accountability for our own sins, the need for personal repentance and faith in the cross and the blood of Jesus. It further attempts to divide and separate us from God's love and forgiveness as well as sow confusion into how we should love one another. It teaches hate and promotes racial division for political gain and power.

Our culture is so saturated with hate, death, and darkness; it truly is alarming. For example, Black Lives Matter, Inc. is a professed Marxist organization. They want to defund the police, burn cities to the ground, and promote violence. They have marched through the streets of America saying things like "Pigs in a blanket, fry them like bacon!" and, "What do we want? Dead cops! When do we want them? Now!" They actively promote the Marxist agenda, and yet some celebrate them as a civil rights organization. Nothing could be further from the truth! BLM actively violates the civil rights of all those who oppose them, regardless of color or gender.

They will say that black lives matter, but if you are a black police officer, your life doesn't. If you are a black conservative, your dignity, civil rights, and character are subject to verbal and physical assault. In reality, *all* black lives matter, from the womb to the tomb. "All Lives Matter" is the counterculture, and we need to mean it.

As I stated earlier, the untimely and unjust killing of George Floyd by a police officer was horrifying, but it doesn't excuse killing police officers and burning down our cities in retaliation. Police reform and addressing the abuse of any citizen of any color is a moral and just demand, but what followed in the name of justice was evil, wrong, and immoral. Any "race based" law enforcement policies must be opposed and reformed.

But it must be done lawfully and peacefully. Martin Luther King, Jr. insisted on peaceful protest and always marched in the daylight. What we see today is evil, violent, and done in the dark. Their deeds are evil, and they won't come to the light. Burning, looting, and harming our fellow citizens and their livelihoods are never justified. I'm in Chicago on a plane as I'm writing this manuscript and it was said to me that crime is up 300 percent in areas where the police have been defunded. The worst part is that the black communities seem to be suffering the most and their lives matter!

Think about how absurd things have become today. If you believe in law and order and equality under the law, you're a racist. If you believe in one national language, two genders, reading, writing, and arithmetic, you're a racist. From elementary school through college, children are taught that if they are white, they are privileged supremacists who contribute to systemic racism. Black children are taught they are "victims." This is beyond absurd and borders on wickedness.

If you think I'm exaggerating or overreacting, consider a display posted at the Smithsonian National Museum of African American History and Culture titled "Aspects & Assumptions of Whiteness and White Culture in the United States." In my opinion, based on biblical principles and Kingdom virtues, this display condemns all resemblance to a civilized and moral society. Here are some of the character traits that are labeled "whiteness": politeness, hard work, self-reliance, logic, planning, and family cohesion. *Wow!* These are all biblical characteristics that mark a loving, productive, civilized, and moral society. They have nothing to do with being white, but everything to do with being godly.

When did being polite and kind become "whiteness" or oppressive? It is a fruit of the Holy Spirit, *not* your color (see Gal. 5:22-23).

When did hard work become oppressive or racist? God said six days we were to work and on the seventh rest (see Exod. 20:8-11). When did self-reliance become an issue of color? God said if anyone doesn't provide for his own, especially those of his own household, he was being worse than an infidel and has denied the faith (see 1 Tim. 5:8). Hard work is God's image in man. God works and we work as a reflection of His image and an expression of His glory, not a statement of one's race. Some scriptures that speak into this are:

If anyone will not work, neither shall he eat.

2 THESSALONIANS 3:10

Let him that stole steal no more: but rather let him labour, working with his hands the thing which is good, that he may have to give to him that needeth.

EPHESIANS 4:28

We work to eat, to have money to give, serve, and support a healthy community. Work and serving is celebrating our humanity while also being a blessing to our fellow man. The family unit, created by God, is not oppressive or "whiteness." God created the family unit consisting of male and female. Jesus addresses this basic truth in Mark 10:2-9 and Genesis 2:18-25. Our gender was created by God (see Gen. 1:26-28) and was intended for marriage and being fruitful in childbearing. Ephesians 6:1-3 commands children to honor and obey father and mother and comes with a promise: that things would go well for us, and we would enjoy long life. What a blessing for all nations of the world.

When one steps back and looks at this belief system, it's easy to see that this is racism, antichrist, and against His Word. However, to oppose it will get you labeled a racist. The accusation of racism has been weaponized to create hate, division, and violence. It is also used to silence any opposition to immorality, perversions, and sin. Unfortunately, when called a racist, many Christians will go stealth regarding their faith and God's righteousness.

The cultural Marxists do not want reconciliation between us. They know that if the races reconciled, we would have civil order, a better society, and a powerful country. The

Marxists can't have that and succeed, so they've made racism the buzz word of the day to divide and conquer. They hate the country, its founders, the Constitution, and they want to destroy it all. Inciting a race war amongst the masses is how they've chosen to do so. For their plan to work, racism must be kept alive, even if they must become racist themselves.

The culture of Marxism is chaos, confusion, division, and hatred, so the counterculture must be one of order, peace, unity, and thanksgiving to God. We look to God, the cross, and God's Word for lasting, eternal, equitable solutions. The simplicity of Jesus resolves our broken and sinful heart condition.

> *But those things which proceed out of the mouth come from the heart, and they defile a man. For out of the heart proceed evil thoughts, murders, adulteries, fornications, thefts, false witness, blasphemies. These are the things which defile a man, but to eat with unwashed hands does not defile a man.*
>
> MATTHEW 15:18-20

This is not an exhaustive list of sins of the heart. Racism is one of many sins that is in the heart of man without God. The problem with man today is his heart. Only God alone can change a man's heart. This is the power of the gospel and the cross (see Rom. 1:16; 1 Cor. 1:18).

In the cultural Marxist world, all social norms are corrupted. The idea of many is that gender is fluid. Family, races, faith, and all aspects of your life are to be questioned and reassigned. If we can alter the norms, we can now benefit all the oppressed groups. Special rights will be awarded to the oppressed. They will not be subject to the same standards or laws to balance the scales.

God's moral law and standards can be canceled out if perceived as oppressive, racist, or sexist. If you are a male and you wake up one day and feel you are a female, the problem is not yours. It is society imposing two genders on us all (iniquity). Now boys can identify as a girl and compete with them in sports and win everything. Once the season of that sport is over, they can be a boy again and be praised for their fluid gender revelation. Never mind the abuse of girls in this scenario. I guess we were all wrong when we passed Title IX helping women rightfully enter into the sports world without discrimination based on gender.

Bathrooms labeled either male or female are now available to anyone of any sexual preference for cross-use based on how they identify at the moment, leaving innocent women and children vulnerable to sexual predators.

OPPRESSED VERSUS OPPRESSORS

Let's break down again who is considered the oppressors versus oppressed. Oppressors are said to be white, native-born males, heterosexual, cisgender Christians. White is the oppressor, black the oppressed. Male is the oppressor, female the oppressed. Heterosexual (sexual orientation that is attracted to the opposite sex) is the oppressor, homosexual (sexual orientation that is attracted to the same sex) the oppressed. Cisgender is the oppressor, transgender (one who does not identify with the sex or gender at his or her birth) the oppressed. Native-born is the oppressor, illegal immigrant the oppressed.

Christians are the oppressors, non-Christians the oppressed. In the light of God's truth, the world has truly gone mad.

Even the foundation of marriage is under assault. To defend it as an institution created by God is offensive and to define it as a covenant between a male and female is oppressive to many. Gay marriage is no longer considered a sin or perversion but just another example of the oppressed gaining their so-called justice. The goal is to destroy what has been normal and godly for thousands of years and rebuild it in man's image. If you can destroy something this basic, what else can we destroy?

Jesus Himself defines marriage and our biological, scientific genders of male and female in Mark 10. When asked specifically on the issue of marriage and divorce, He addresses why God created us male and female. He explains why God allowed divorce even though it was never His will:

> And Jesus answered and said to them, "Because of the hardness of your heart he [Moses] wrote you this precept. But from the beginning of the creation God 'made them male and female.' 'For this reason a man shall leave his father and mother and be joined to his wife, and the two shall become one flesh'; so then they are no longer two, but one flesh. Therefore what God has joined together, let not man separate."
>
> MARK 10:5-9

Jesus addresses the purpose for male and female, the two genders God created. It was for marriage! Any marriage outside of male and female is a perversion. Something as simple as God creating our gender is now oppressive. God created marriage and defined it. God creates our gender assignment. Your very DNA (science) testifies of your gender, yet an entire generation is being taught gender confusion, which is corrupting the basic concept of marriage.

Every cell in your body is a witness of your gender. Your blood carries your genetic code of either male (sex chromosome XY) or female (sex chromosome XX). Life is in the blood, and it cannot lie. The blood that runs through your veins testifies of your life and gender.

For the life of the flesh is in the blood.

LEVITICUS 17:11

But flesh with the life thereof, which is the blood.

GENESIS 9:4

Everything is under assault because the goal of the Marxist is to "tear it all down" in "the Revolution." This is all out of the Karl Marx playbook and is militant Marxism. Remember that Marxism and communism are atheistic systems, so God must be removed from society, period. If what God says about any subject is rejected, then it can be torn down and a man-made system of justice and equity can be erected in its place.

Even our black brothers and sisters are attacked and called "white supremacists" if they don't comply with CRT. In September 2021, CNN's website posted an article titled "White Supremacy with a Tan,"[2] which attacks any black person who does not buy into the CRT narrative. How insidious! How depraved does someone have to become before their opinions are no longer taken seriously? Any black person who does not drink the Kool-Aid of CRT is said to be "not really black" but is rather a "white supremacist."

Even our color is now being defined by our ideology. We must wake up to this kind of evil before it's too late. This is the new "intolerance movement" in America, the epitome of the cancel culture even to the canceling of our own color! Proponents of CRT and evidently some at CNN promote division over friendship, hostility rather than goodwill, hate rather than love, tear it down rather than build it up better. It is classical Marxism that is headed toward "the Revolution" *not* "reconciliation." What's next?

TRUE RECONCILIATION

The counterculture is one where all men and women are created equal, and there is no division between the races in Christ because we are all of one blood and worldwide nation (Acts 17:26). Reconciliation cannot be attained through man's philosophies or government programs because true reconciliation comes through Christ Jesus and the cross. While I can acknowledge transgressions of the past, I'm not guilty of my father's sins:

> *The fathers shall not be put to death for the children, neither shall the children be put to death for the fathers; every man shall be put to death for his own sin.*
>
> DEUTERONOMY 24:16

We are all accountable before God for our sins and not the sins of others. I'm only held accountable by God for other's sins when I don't warn them of the consequences of sin (see Chapter 14). I don't need to be compelled to confess to white supremacy because I am certain, in my heart, I do not believe that whites are superior to blacks or any other race.

> *God is no respecter of persons.*
>
> ACTS 10:34

I don't have to confess that I have white privilege because I have the blessing of Abraham on my life.

> *Christ has redeemed us from the curse of the law, having become a curse for us...that the blessing of Abraham might come upon the Gentiles in Christ Jesus, that we might receive the promise of the Spirit through faith.*
>
> GALATIANS 3:13-14

We are all blessed with this blessing of Abraham because of grace and faith.

> *For you know the grace of our Lord Jesus Christ, that though He was rich, yet for your sakes He became poor, that you through His poverty might become rich.*
>
> 2 CORINTHIANS 8:9

Grace and peace have been multiplied unto us through the knowledge of God and Jesus our Lord:

> *According as his divine power hath given unto us all things that pertain unto life and godliness.*
>
> 2 PETER 1:3

The sacrifice of Jesus on the cross has provided this. That divine power mentioned above is the amazing grace of our Lord Jesus and is available to all the races of the world. Grace, not race, has provided God's riches and blessing for all of us. There is no discrimination in the cross.

I have no need for Critical Race Theory and can clearly see the wrong of soft bigotry concerning low expectations of an entire group of people. All of us are well able to prosper on our own through Christ and the cross—no matter what our race, gender, or social status is.

> *And you shall remember the Lord your God, for it is*
> *He who gives you power to get wealth.*
>
> DEUTERONOMY 8:18

My black brothers and sisters are complete in Christ and do not require confessions of sins committed by past generations (see Col. 2:10). Again, in the counterculture, we look to the gospel for reconciliation.

> *That is, that God was in Christ reconciling the world*
> *to Himself, not imputing their trespasses to them,*
> *and has committed to us the word of reconcilia-*
> *tion. Now then, we are ambassadors for Christ, as*
> *though God were pleading through us: we implore*
> *you on Christ's behalf, be reconciled to God.*
>
> 2 CORINTHIANS 5:19-20

The call for reconciliation is to God and then one another. It is the ministry God has given every believer to share with the world. We are the ambassadors God is sending and the cross is the center of the message. As long as men refuse to be reconciled to God, divisions among men will remain.

> *For you are all sons of God through faith in Christ*
> *Jesus. For as many of you as were baptized into*

Christ have put on Christ. There is neither Jew nor Greek, there is neither slave nor free, there is neither male nor female; for you are all one in Christ Jesus.

GALATIANS 3:26-28

All divisions, created by sin in the world, are reconciled in Christ. All our differences are overcome by putting on Christ. Furthermore, if the divisions between Jew and Gentile, male and female, bond or free are torn down by the cross and new birth (new creation)—then black and white has been torn down as well. It is the world and philosophies of the world that divide the races, not the counterculture.

Paul (a Jew) wrote to Christian Gentiles:

But now in Christ Jesus you who once were far off have been brought near by the blood of Christ. For He Himself is our peace, who has made both one, and has broken down the middle wall of separation, having abolished in His flesh the enmity, that is, the law of commandments contained in ordinances, so as to create in Himself one new man from the two, thus making peace, and that He might reconcile them both to God in one body through the cross, thereby putting to death the enmity. And He came and preached peace to you who were afar off and to those who were near. For through Him we both have access by one Spirit to the Father.

EPHESIANS 2:13-18

During this time, there was no greater division than that of Jew and Gentile. That division was mended and healed by the cross. Anything that separates us is torn down by the cross, and the blood of Jesus makes us all one in Christ. The culture of Marxism says the answer to our social problems is socialism, gender fluid acceptance, normalized sexual perversion, new age philosophies, radical feminism, and CRT. The Spirit-filled culture cannot embrace these counterfeit solutions that are enemies of the cross. People who believe in the cultural Marxist theories are deceived. This is a false hope that people put trust in. Our hope is in Jesus and His Kingdom. The counterculture has the love of God shed in our hearts by the Holy Spirit (see Rom. 5:5), and because of that there is no room for racism, bigotry, or hate—only a heart that loves God and His people.

While those in the world are trying to obtain reconciliation and unity among the races by carnal means, the church has been called to maintain the unity we already have in the Spirit. In Ephesians 4:1-3, Paul is encouraging believers to:

> *Walk worthy of the calling with which you were called, with all lowliness and gentleness, with long-suffering, bearing with one another in love, endeavoring to keep the unity of the Spirit in the bond of peace.*

Endeavoring simply means "to work at, to make effort, be prompt, diligent, labor" (*spoudazo*, Strong's G4704). As Christians, we must be prompt and diligent to *keep* the unity of the Spirit, which simply means we stand in the finished work of the cross and God's amazing grace. Christ has made us one in Him, and the bond of peace provided by the cross is what we labor to maintain, not have to obtain.

If someone says, "I love God," and hates his brother, he is a liar; for he who does not love his brother whom he has seen, how can he love God whom he has not seen? And this commandment we have from Him: that he who loves God must love his brother also.

1 JOHN 4:20-21

We know that we have passed from death to life, because we love the brethren. He who does not love his brother abides in death.

1 JOHN 3:14

Those who hate and teach hate are not of God. They abide in death and are liars according to the Scriptures. Those who follow the counterculture, love their brothers regardless of race, gender, or outward appearance. Man may judge on outer appearance, but God looks on the heart (see 1 Sam. 16:7). May our hearts be cleansed and purified from all forms of racism and bigotry. May we be awakened to the antichrist evil of Marxism. May our loyalty to Christ and His Kingdom be renewed.

Grace and the cross remain the hope and healing of the nation. May *Critical Grace Theory* dominate the counterculture.

NOTES

1. "Critical Race Theory: A Bait and Switch Tactic Infiltrating the Church," qtd. in Lighthouse Trails Research Project, December 2, 2019, https://www.lighthousetrailsresearch .com/blog/?p=31044.

2. John Blake, "White supremacy, with a tan," CNN, September 4, 2021, https://www.cnn.com/2021/09/04/us/census -browning-of-america-myth-blake/index.html.

CHAPTER 12

SOCIALISM AND COMMUNISM

Socialism is the transition from capitalism to communism.
—KARL MARX

The whole history of socialism… is…revolutionary striving. The goal of socialism is communism.
—VLADIMIR LENIN, Founder of the Russian Communist Party

In 1945, English author George Orwell wrote a book titled *Animal Farm*. It was about a poorly run manor farm near Wellington, England. This farm is ripened for rebellion from the animals because of neglect at the hands of the irresponsible and alcoholic farmer Mr. Jones. The animals simply overthrow the farmer and set up their own system of governance. They

start out with promises of equality, equity, and justice. "All animals are equal" is the original declaration.

A pig named Napoleon rises to power, and the pigs soon become the ruling class. They get the best food and supplies while the other animals get the leftovers. The farm soon deteriorates to the "ruling class" versus the "ruled class." The mantra becomes, "All animals are equal, but some animals are more equal than others." Napoleon and his lynch animals become corrupt and brutal. They begin lying to others to cover up all their corruption. They blame others falsely for their evil ways, making themselves out to be the good guys and saviors of all the animals. The story ends with an unholy alliance with the humans where everyone is corrupt, lying, and cheating, and they all know it. This was a satire slap at communism during that time, yet it still remains so today. It has been said of old, "Power corrupts, and absolute power corrupts absolutely."

We cannot give up our "so called" freedoms in the name of social justice, equity, fairness, or sameness, knowing what the outcome would be. Socialism, increasingly popular among many of our young people, is becoming a legitimate threat to our freedom. Even worse, it is affecting the church, even though it is not rooted in Kingdom principles and biblical truth. Where is a generation going to hear the truth if not from the church?

IT'S FREE!?

With socialism comes the promise of "everything free"— free housing, free health care, a universal paycheck, debt forgiveness from student loans to mortgages paid off and more. However, nothing is free, and we cannot afford to pay the price that socialism requires. When we give government any kind of power over our lives, we are giving away our sovereignty.

In his 1974 joint session of Congress, President Gerald Ford said, "A government big enough to give you everything you want is a government big enough to take from you everything you have." In a speech at the Southern Methodist University's Autumn Convocation, Gerald Ford also said, "Never forget that in America, our Sovereign is the citizen; Government and institutions exist to serve the people. The State is the servant of the individual. It must never become an anonymous monstrosity that masters everyone and is responsive to no one."[1]

Many of our leaders of the past saw the danger of an overreaching, all-powerful government. The founding fathers of our country saw it, so they gave us our original documents to restrict it and to protect the individual from abusive government—namely, the Declaration of Independence, the Constitution, and the Bill of Rights. So few see it today and those who do are attacked, censored, or canceled.

In July 2009, the Speaker of the House, Nancy Pelosi, and a group of Democrats introduced the Affordable Care Act (Obamacare) to Congress for consideration. When questioned about what was in the bill, Pelosi said, "We have to pass the bill to see what's in it!"[2] Wow, that's alarming! She would not divulge the contents of the bill until it was passed. Several months later, without a clear explanation of the quality of care we would receive, Barack Obama signed the ACA into law in March of 2010. This "free healthcare" was made to sound so good and beneficial to each citizen.

LIES UPON LIES

However, it soon became clear that we were lied to. The families that were promised free and affordable health care couldn't find clinics that could see them without a long wait and could not afford the most basic medications like insulin. Fast-forward to 2020 when COVID-19 hit our world and we really got to see what happens when we put our government in charge of our health.

First, we were told we could flatten the curve and save lives if we shut down and quarantined for two short weeks. Wow, that now seems like ages ago. Then face masks were enforced with the threat of fines levied if not obeyed. Businesses and schools were then forced to remain closed, and continued quarantines were mandated.

Now we have vaccine passports in some countries, and even in some of our own states you cannot go anywhere unless you have been "vaccinated" against COVID. Technically it is not a vaccination but rather a shot. It started off as two doses, but now they are saying a third booster shot will be needed. Kind of sounds like the two-week shutdown lie. Many people are just doing what they're told because the government said so.

At the writing of this book, our government is mandating multiple rounds of a COVID-19 vaccine plus boosters for all federal employees, the entire military, private businesses with more than 100 employees, and contractors doing business with government. Some local governments are requiring vaccine IDs to be able to gather at bars, eat at restaurants, shop, or visit public venues. The list goes on with discussions concerning a required vaccine passport in order to buy, sell, trade, or travel in any capacity. Sound familiar?

> *He causes all, both small and great, rich and poor, free and slave, to receive a mark on their right hand or on their foreheads, and that no one may buy or sell except one who has the mark or the name of the beast, or the number of his name.*
>
> REVELATION 13:16-17

They say that all of this is for the good of our society. However, what is happening behind the scenes is anything but good for us. Nations and wealthy elite leaders are using this crisis for a worldwide "Great Reset." In the "Great Reset" there will be worldwide mandates in the name of our healthcare. COVID hysteria, climate change, and endless manufactured crises are still being systematically deployed to take control of every aspect of our lives. "Comply or die" is just around the corner.

Great fear has been generated through COVID-19— even though it is a virus with a 99 percent survival rate. Yet because of media in all forms broadcasting the direst of consequences from contracting this virus, most Americans are so scared that they have accepted unreasonable demands of unprecedented shutdowns and quarantines and vaccine mandates.

During the 2020 national election, people even let the politicians leverage our health for political gain as well. For example, it was okay to go to Walmart in person, but voting in person was considered to be a super-spreader event. They pushed mail-in voting on us for the sake of our communities. Mass mail-in voting is just a recipe for fraud.

Censorship is at an all-time high. Harry Truman is quoted as saying, "Communism subjects the individual to arrest without lawful cause, punishment without trial, and forced labor as a chattel (slave) of the state...It declares what information a person shall receive, what art they shall produce, what leader they shall follow, and what thoughts they shall think."[3]

Wow, does any of this sound familiar? The cancel culture in the arena of social media is determining what information is posted and distributed. During COVID-19, the government was telling us what jobs were "essential" and those that were not! Our national media is in bed with the "Great Reset" agenda and censors all news and information to achieve their desired outcome. If it hurts their opponents, it is front and center for days. If it portrays their allies in a bad light, it is buried and to uncover it would make you a "conspiracy theorist."

If the current level of fear, confusion, and hysteria around COVID ever wanes, it will rapidly shift to another more frightening crises like a deadlier variant outbreak, a bio-weapon attack, climate change on steroids, or you name it. Whether perceived or real, if enough people in darkness continue to be enslaved by this onslaught of fear, can you imagine what they might allow to be imposed on them next? We must peacefully and lovingly resist in faith before it's too late.

Let's take a moment to ask some simple questions:

- What will be your real cost for all those "free things" the government promised you?

- What will be your personal sacrifice to save the planet? Your life? Your liberty?

- If the government cancels all student loan debt, say goodbye to choosing quality education. If students don't pay, who does? You and me! I have no desire to pay for young people to be taught to hate their country, renounce their faith in God, and embrace socialism. I am not obligated to pay for hate, death, and darkness to be taught.

- What happens if we let the government absorb our mortgage debt? We lose our private property.

Many people believe that we should all have universal paychecks. That will cost them free commerce and privately owned businesses. Universal free healthcare was never about the sick or poor and having so-called compassion. If the government can control healthcare, then they can control your lives. They can declare "essential" and "non-essential" occupations. They can limit who will travel and who will be quarantined. The ultimate goal of socialism is not to help the poor. It has always been and will always be to eliminate capitalism and transition us into communism. It is all about enriching and empowering the few at the expense of the masses.

Under socialism and communism, private ownership of property, land, and business shifts from the private sector to big government placing a stranglehold on free and open markets with stifling regulations that implode the economy. The ownership of land and private business are both biblical principles, not secular greedy dreams.

God gave Abraham land and blessed his herds and commerce. The Scriptures declare that he became very rich in cattle, in silver, and in gold (see Gen. 13:1). Israel was given land, and regardless of whether they sold it or lost it through poor stewardship, they got it back every 50 years, the year of Jubilee (see Lev. 25:8-16).

In Acts 4 and 5, families sold land and gave to the church. The church did not take their land but rather received it because it was freely given, and that is genuine compassion. King David bought a threshing floor from a citizen named Araunah to offer sacrifices to God (see 2 Sam. 24:21-24). Deuteronomy 8:18 says it is God who gives us the power to gain wealth and establish His covenant.

Socialism and communism will tell you that they distribute wealth equally. The annals of history record the disaster that follows these philosophies, yet some believe that if the right people get in charge with the right amount of money, it will work. It's just not true. Socialism will never work because it violates our faith, personal responsibility, and accountability. It robs the human soul of any just rewards for hard work, innovation, and servanthood. It uses extortion and calls it compassion, equity, and justice. It takes from producers and gives to non-producers, creating a dependency class.

It truly is the spirit of antichrist and the epitome of greed and covetousness, which is idolatry (see Col. 3:5). Unfortunately, the church doesn't recognize this spirit and is as easily deceived as the world. Not everything that sounds good is good!

JUSTICE

Another false promise of socialism and communism is justice for all. Equity, fairness, and social justice are the bait on the hook that ensnares the innocent, unsuspecting fish. Who is going to oppose any of those noble qualities? We must be a people of justice in defending the poor, weak, and disadvantaged among us, right? The problem is that socialism and communism approach these issues from the Garden of Eden paradigm. It believes that man can achieve these lofty goals without God. All kinds of unrighteousness and injustice is committed in the name of justice—trying to legislate and then intimidate people into being and doing good. Love forced or mandated is not love at all. Compassion and love are acts of man's heart and freewill.

Socialism and communism believe the government gets to decide what it means to be good and will use violence to enforce their interpretations if they feel the need. Socialism eats of the forbidden tree of the knowledge of good and evil. Like Adam, it believes that we can know what's good and evil independent of God, the only One good. God would have taught Adam what is good and evil in time as they walked together in the cool of the day.

Man without God calls good evil and evil good, light darkness and darkness light (see Isa. 5:20). There is no one good but God, Jesus said (see Matt. 19:17). We cannot know, be, or do good without God! Any good in our lives is the image of God who deserves all praise and glory.

In today's culture you can see the result of man determining good and evil apart from God. Pure evil is celebrated in many of our institutions today. Everything is completely upside down. Sexual perversion is paraded in our streets with great pride. Sexual purity is mocked and sneered at. God's righteousness is called hate speech while true hate speech is echoed on the six o'clock news and, unfortunately, on many of our college campuses. While God is blessing the nations, many college professors are tearing ours down. Man is declared good without God and men of God are mocked, prosecuted, and persecuted.

Look at our ruling class right now—they go out to eat and host massive birthday parties with their friends and families, but we are forced to stay home. They go without masks while you can be fined for not wearing one. They can opt out of vaccines, but many are being forced to take them if they want to work. It is a "good for thee, but not me" mentality. Like in *Animal Farm*, those in government are becoming the ruling class and those who are not are becoming the ruled class. They are exercising absolute power over us and are expecting us to comply without question. The double standards are glaring, the hypocrisy overwhelming, the inequities front and center, and the darkness blinding.

Our Judeo-Christian values established this great nation, and our elected officials were there to serve us and represent our best interests. We were to be the masters and they the servants. Get rid of God and that will always be reversed. That is the nature of man without God. This is not good, and a government without God will always lead to no good. I'm not against government. God has ordained and established government among men (see Rom. 13:1). I'm against corrupt government or one that is atheistic telling the church what and who is good. Jeremiah 17:9-10 says:

> *The heart is deceitful above all things, and desperately wicked; who can know it? I, the Lord, search the heart, I test the mind, even to give every man according to his ways, according to the fruit of his doings.*

Without God, man is deceitful and wicked of heart; how much more are government systems that reject God. Jesus said out of men's hearts proceed *"evil thoughts, murders, adulteries, fornications, thefts, false witness, blasphemies. These are the things which defile a man"* (Matt. 15:19-20).

No matter how our government packages what they're doing, committing acts of unrighteousness in the name of justice or our health is evil. Justice without God's sound judgment turns into violence and vigilantism. Vigilantism brings the sound of mourning and pain with tears, because justice that harms its fellow man and commits acts of unrighteousness is a perversion. Socialism and communism offer the false hope of solutions but come with a price. They are counterfeits and opponents to Christ, the Messiah. That puts them in direct association with the spirit of antichrist.

In 1950 during a speech given to his attorneys general, Harry Truman said, "If we don't have a proper fundamental moral background, we will finally end up with a totalitarian government which does not believe in the rights of anybody except for the state."[4] How do we combat these evil ideologies? Well, the counterculture to socialism and communism is one with a proper moral background that can only be found in God.

> *He has shown you, O man, what is good; and what*
> *does the Lord require of you but to do justly, to love*
> *mercy, and to walk humbly with your God?*
>
> MICAH 6:8

Notice it is God who has shown us what it good. We must do justly and love mercy, while remaining humble before God.

As a Christian leader, I consider it a privilege to call for justice and equity in our social interactions as human beings created in God's image. God's justice is pure, righteous, and fair. It is unbiased; has no prejudice; is no respecter of color, gender, financial condition, or political power (see Acts 10:34). We are all equal under God and under the law.

> *But the Lord sits enthroned forever; he has estab-*
> *lished his throne for justice, and he judges the*
> *world with righteousness; he judges the peoples*
> *with uprightness.*
>
> PSALM 9:7-8 (ESV)

God's justice is righteous and treats our fellow man honorably. God chose Abraham to be the father of many nations because he would "*command his children and his household after him, and they shall keep the way of the Lord, to do justice and* judgment" (Gen. 18:19).

Notice the connection with justice and judgment. *Judgment* in the Hebrew language means "divine law" to judge or pronounce a sentence (*misshpat*, Strong's H4941). With God's justice, morality is fundamental in the actions of and sentencing of a guilty party. In other words, you cannot execute justice in an evil or unjust way or it's no longer justice. The New King James version reads, *"command his children and his household after him, that they keep the way of the Lord, to do righteousness and justice."*

David was a great king because he *"executed judgment and justice unto all his people"* (2 Sam. 8:15; see also 1 Kings 10:9; 1 Chron. 18:14; 2 Chron. 9:8).

> *Righteousness and justice are the foundation of Your throne; mercy and truth go before Your face. Blessed are the people who know the joyful sound!*
>   PSALM 89:14-15

Notice again the connection of righteousness and justice. Separating "do what's right" from "justice" perverts God's justice. Mercy and truth are vital to God's kind of justice. In Galatians 3:26-28 (NLT), we see our equality in Jesus:

> *For you are all children of God through faith in Christ Jesus. And all who have been united with Christ in baptism have put on Christ, like putting on new clothes. There is no longer Jew or Gentile, slave or free, male and female. For you are all one in Christ Jesus.*

Socialism and communism seek to enforce what they perceive as just and equitable the wrong way. Through Jesus and the work of the cross, God has made us all one in Jesus— equally loved, blessed, forgiven, and changed in our hearts. Socialism and communism seek to enforce man's justice resulting in bias and injustice.

Russian immigrant and writer Ayn Rand wrote: "There is no difference between communism and socialism except in the means of achieving the same ultimate end. Communism proposes to enslave men by force, socialism by vote. It is merely the difference between murder and suicide."[5]

In socialism there are an elite few who think they are wiser and smarter than God and the average citizen. They think they can govern themselves and others without God. They create crises in order to create fear. With the government's promise of protection, citizens slowly and gradually yield their freedom over to the state. There is usually a party or group that now cares for the citizen and does their thinking for them.

The state becomes sovereign, and the citizen becomes subjugated. The state becomes the master and you become the slave. They empower themselves by convincing you to hand over your power to them through false promises and fear campaigns. Socialism is established through ballots (votes), communism by bullets (force); the end is death of liberty. They are an atheistic form of government. Without God they can't even know good or evil, righteousness, equity, or justice.

There must be a counterculture to the culture of socialism before it has a chance to usher communism through the door. There must be peaceful pushback and loving accountability before it is too late. Socialism promises what only can be found in Jesus, the cross, and the Kingdom of God.

It is my prayer that the counterculture be awakened and shine the light on the loss of freedom and the overreach of abusive government. Thank God for light (truth) and children of light speaking out! Because of them and with God's help, the best is yet to come.

NOTES

1. Gerald Ford, "Address at a Southern Methodist University Convocation," The American Presidency Project, 1975, https://www.presidency.ucsb.edu/node/257408.

2. Nancy Pelosi, "Pelosi Remarks at the 2010 Legislative Conference for National Association of Counties," Press Release, 2010, https://pelosi.house.gov/news/press-releases/pelosi-remarks-at-the-2010-legislative-conference-for-national-association-of.

3. Harry Truman, "Inaugural Address," The American Presidency Project, 2021, https://www.presidency.ucsb.edu/documents/inaugural-address-4.

4. Harry Truman qtd. in William Federer, "Harry S Truman's Role in World War I, in Creating New State of Israel, & in Warning of Anarchy Leading to Dictatorship," American Minute with Bill Federer, 2021, https://americanminute.com/blogs/todays-american-minute/harry-s-trumans-role-in-world-war-i-in-creating-new-state-of-israel-and-in-warning-of-anarchy-leading-to-dictatorship-american-minute-with-bill-federer.

5. Ayn Rand, "Totalitarian Communism & State Socialism, Voting & Democracy," The Los Angeles Times, 1962.

CHAPTER 13

WE THE PEOPLE

Let every soul be subject to the governing authorities. For there is no authority except from God, and the authorities that exist are appointed by God.
—ROMANS 13:1

The disrespect we see today against all forms of authority is not godly. Government is a part of all civil societies. We will be governed by some form of government, either by choice or default. We are blessed beyond measure to have a form of government that is rooted in Judeo-Christian principles and values but also protects the rights of individuals versus the power of government that historically can become abusive. It's important to understand that I'm not against government; I'm against corrupt government.

Ancient Israel rejected God as their King and insisted on having a king like all the other nations (see 1 Sam. 8:5-6). Samuel explained to them what sorrows would come to them in having a king besides God (see 1 Sam. 8:11-22). However, the Israelites remained steadfast in their rebellion. Even after God warned them of the pain and sorrows that natural kings would bring, they refused to repent of this idolatry and desire to be like other nations.

For thousands of years man has been ruled and abused by kings, lords, dictators, tyrants, and despots. Poverty for the masses has been the common lot, while greed, exorbitant wealth, and power are for the few. The leaders were sovereign over who they led. The leaders were the masters and the people slaves.

The beauty and majesty of our founders was the idea of "we the people," not "they the government" or "me the king." We became the sovereign and master of the leaders. In a democratic, representative republic we are empowered to elect who rules over us. We get to hire or fire the elected officials (see Exod. 18:14-24). The Constitution of the United States of America protects us from abusive politicians, not them from us. It limits government on what they can or cannot do to us. Thank You, Jesus!

God ordained government, but not ungodly, abusive government. While God ordains government, not every person in government is ordained of God or follows His will and shouldn't be followed independent of our free will. The same can be said of the kings of Israel. Not all of them were put in authority by God. In Hosea 8:3-4, God said that Israel put these ungodly kings over them:

Israel hath cast off the thing that is good: the enemy shall pursue him. They have set up kings, but not by me: they have made princes, and I knew it not: of their silver and their gold have they made them idols, that they may be cut off.

Many lives have been destroyed throughout history by corrupt governments that have created poverty and famine for the masses. Most of the human suffering throughout the world today can be laid at the feet of immoral, ungodly, corrupt government. Leaders enrich and empower themselves at the cost of human lives. From Mao of communist China to Pol Pot of Cambodia, history is filled with human suffering at the hands of dictators. Hitler of Nazi Germany destroyed millions of lives. Joseph Stalin starved his own people by the millions. We must elect godly people into office to stay free and continue in God's blessing. The story of humanity for millennia has been people are born free (God-given right) only to be enslaved by selfish, power-hungry, evil men and women (corrupt governments).

Our form of government, made up of three different branches, comes from the Bible. It limits abusive powers and keeps the powerful accountable.

For the Lord is our Judge, the Lord is our Lawgiver, the Lord is our King; he will save us.
ISAIAH 33:22

Our judge (judicial branch), our lawgiver (house and senate), and our king (executive branch)—these three work in perfect harmony within God. Much like all three members of the Godhead are co-equal, these branches of government are also. This is what is meant by Judeo-Christian principles. These fundamentals come from or have their origin in Scripture—either from the Old Testament or New Testament.

Corrupt government is a part of the culture of hate, death, and darkness. There is a hate for freedom and individual liberty. There is a death of freedom slowly occurring as we continue to elect people who hate God. There is a culture of darkness invading our politics as we continue to believe lies and reject truth. A part of the great awakening is a return to constitutional government and public policies that are rooted in Judeo-Christian values and principles, not Marxism.

AMERICAN EXCEPTIONALISM

Freedom is a gift from God. It is not the natural order of things in a world without God. The whole world is in darkness, and tyranny is the result of that darkness. Freedom is the overflow of the gospel (see Gal. 5:1). The Kingdom of God is one of freedom and allegiance to Jesus and His Lordship. The Kingdom of God (light) promotes freedom, while the kingdoms of this world (darkness) impose bondage. Our freedom is not a benevolent act of government, but rather a divine gift from God. What makes America exceptional is freedom. We are born free and promised by God to remain free people.

This birthright is enshrined in our Constitution. We are exceptional not because of the land or the color of our skin or the blood in our veins, but the ring of freedom in our hearts. We are exceptional because of founding fathers who made a way in our Constitution to be able to amend it to address injustice that sin and Satan afflicted upon the fallen world. It was to be amended as this country grew and progressed in order to deal with new issues that would arise, though always with the intent of serving mankind rather than harming them. It is, and we are, exceptional because when we fall short of our ideals, we can address them by ballots and not bullets.

We are exceptional because we can be a city set on a hill and an encouragement to the nations of the world of the power of freedom. We are exceptional because we have a society based on the rule of law, not the rule of men. We are to strive to measure up to the ideals enumerated within our founding documents as well as the Holy Scriptures. When we fall short (and we often do) we are to repent and seek God's forgiveness and wisdom on how to govern and be governed as a free people.

> AMERICANS ARE EXCEPTIONAL NOT BECAUSE OF THE LAND, THE COLOR OR OUR SKIN, OR THE BLOOD IN OUR VEINS—BUT BECAUSE OF THE RING OF FREEDOM IN OUR HEARTS.

A brief and simple overview of our founding documents—the Declaration, the Constitution, the Bill of Rights—reveals the beauty and wisdom of our Constitution and a representative republic. The founders knew that freedom was not the natural order of things but a gift from God. Freedom is achieved and maintained when the light of the gospel is proclaimed. In a world without Christ there is darkness. It is that darkness that allows tyranny to spread. The light of the gospel sets the captives free.

Knowing the dangers of tyranny firsthand, our nation's founders enshrined our God-given birthright of freedom into the Constitution, publicly acknowledging God's "unalienable rights" for everyone. It is this document that makes us different from every other nation. Even at the time of writing the Constitution, they knew that they would leave important details out, so they made a way to amend their vision. Many of our current officials would have you believe that it is our wokeness that makes us exceptional. That is simply not true.

DECLARATION OF INDEPENDENCE

"We hold these truths to be self-evident, that all men are created equal, that they are endowed by their Creator with certain unalienable rights, that among these are life, liberty, and the pursuit of happiness."

This founding document declares our equality before God and is a moral standard we should all strive for. Any injustice that violates this needs to be addressed and reversed. A nation under God would strive for the reality of our equal value and worth before God. Human life is sacred under God from the womb to the tomb.

Abraham Lincoln's justification of the Civil War was based on the Bible and this document. The Bible and this document demand all men be free. While the southern colonies were not exclusive in their heinous sin of slavery, it is the Bible and the Declaration of Independence that made Americans responsible for ending the practice. Over 600,000 lives were lost and sacrificed for the just cause of freedom.

Our Constitution is not the problem now, nor was it then. The Civil War did not have to occur had we followed Scripture and our Constitution. Evil men will not honor either one. Lincoln realized that we were in rebellion to God and betraying our highest ideals. Those who teach and declare that our Constitution is a racist document have not read it or choose to ignore the biblical and godly moral standards it was written upon.

Abortion is a sin of the world, and I believe we will see this crime against the most vulnerable and innocent among us reversed. The Declaration of Independence declares that our freedoms come from God, not government (certain truths are "self-evident"). That means anyone with a conscience that's not been seared with a hot iron and dulled by sin knows them and understands that all lives matter. No one is better or worse in the eyes of a righteous, just, and holy God.

We've all sinned and come short of the glory of God (see Rom. 3:23). There is no one righteous without God, and He considers our self-righteousness as filthy rags (see Isa. 64:6-7). We all need a savior and are equally guilty before God. We all are equally saved and made righteous in His eyes by grace and faith. We are all equally sinners without God and equally made righteous with God.

We are also "endowed by our Creator," not government. This document affirms that our rights come from God and not man. Marxism and communism grant to the people what they determine is a citizen's right. In a culture of fraud and deceit, our founding fathers are constantly impugned and called all kinds of derogatory names. They are said to not be Christians or have faith. It is a true statement that not all the founders were Christians. They were not all born-again, Spirit-filled believers. They were mere people and as flawed as the writer and reader of this book. I hope that hit you as hard as it did me! We are all flawed and fall short of God's glory.

But notice the positive effect Christianity had on them all in forming a document signed by all acknowledging a Creator. Acknowledging the existence of God and His divine providence in the affairs of man doesn't make you a Christian, but it does speak of a fear (reverence) of God. Notice the reference to "unalienable rights." This means it doesn't come from man, so it cannot be taken away by man. Our freedom as a birthright comes from God. It was bequeathed to us by the founders who received it from God.

When we defend freedom, we are being spiritual, not carnal. We are honoring God, not man. We are a counterculture. The goal of all this anti-American rhetoric and declaring the Constitution to be a racist document is to tear it all down—thus "the Revolution." Many want to overthrow our system of government and replace it. With what? I can just about guarantee that it will not be rooted in Judeo-Christian principles and morals.

What are these rights from God? Life, liberty, and the pursuit of happiness. When we defend these, we are being a counterculture to socialism, tyranny, government overreach, and communism as a godless system of government. Freedom is rooted in God Himself. The principles and values of Scripture form a culture in opposition to death, tyranny, and antichrist. Good governance is rooted in moral absolutes and in Kingdom principles that glorify Jesus. Remove God and you lose freedom.

> *Blessed is the nation whose God is the Lord, the people He has chosen as His own inheritance.*
>
> PSALM 33:12

Our blessings as a nation are from God. A nation cannot be blessed if it rejects God. To reject God in choosing Marxism, socialism, and communism is to receive a curse.

> *All nations whom thou hast made shall come and worship before thee, O Lord; and shall glorify thy name.*
>
> PSALM 86:9

This was a call to the nations, not just individuals. God loves the nations, and I believe ours is one that has been called to be a blessing to all other nations of the world.

> *Righteousness exalteth a nation: but sin is a reproach to any people.*
>
> PROVERBS 14:34

Unrighteousness is what brings nations down. We are called to make disciples of nations (see Matt. 28:18-20). To disciple is to teach our nation the foundational truths of God's Word.

OUR CONSTITUTION

"We the people of the United States, in order to form a more perfect union, establish justice, ensure domestic tranquility, provide for the common defense, promote the general welfare, and secure the blessing of liberty to ourselves and our posterity, do ordain and establish this Constitution of the United States of America."

Preamble to the Constitution

Our Constitution was ordained to set a people on a path of governance that would please almighty God. It protects individual sovereignty, dignity, freedom, and protection from tyrannical governments, kings, and lords of the past. It outlines our basic Christian faith in the importance of justice being established in a civil, God-fearing society. Its intent was to lay the foundation to form a more perfect union. It was not declaring we are a perfect union, but rather with God's help and pursuit of Him, we would be a "more perfect union."

In securing the "blessing of liberty" for themselves and future generations, freedom would pave the way for God and a moral people to be a blessing to others. They knew that generational prosperity would be connected to freedom. It includes our Bill of Rights with its first 10 amendments and 27 ratified amendments. The Constitution is made up of seven articles. The Bill of Rights protects the individual from abuse of power within government. The amendments and articles restrict the nature of "man without God" to lord over the masses.

The First Amendment

The first amendment protects the most basic and important right of a free people. It prevents the government from making laws that regulate an establishment of religion, or that would prohibit the free exercise of religion or abridge the freedom of speech, the freedom of the press, the freedom of assembling, or the right to petition the government for redress of grievances. *Wow!* What a blessing!

Those are rooted in God and the freedom to seek, serve, and worship Him without persecution, prosecution, or execution from the government. What a blessed country we live in to serve God according to His Word plus the right to assemble and worship God as conscience and Scripture dictate. No king, dictator, despot, or tyrant would have allowed all of that.

God is using COVID-19 to uncover government overreach in shutting places of worship down. Without freedom, the Constitution, and those willing to defend it, we would be forbidden to assemble, Bibles would be burned, and Christians censored, persecuted, prosecuted, and even executed for the faith. We see this in other parts of the world where they are not free. This assessment is not an exaggeration or extreme. People in gulags or reeducation camps believed it couldn't happen to them.

AN EAGLE

The eagle is our national symbol. There are two wings that cause an eagle to soar. The Declaration of Independence is one wing and the Constitution the other, causing us as a nation to soar like the eagle in prosperity and blessings. The Declaration declares our "equality under God"—the first of the two wings. The Constitution declares our "equality under the law"—the second wing. When these work in tandem, we will remain a "civil" and "free" people maintaining our God-given prosperity. The Constitution is our *birthright* as an American citizen. The Kingdom of God is my birthright (new birth) as a Christian. I received these two birthrights by God's grace and my faith.

God was displeased with Esau for rejecting his birthright (see Heb. 12:14-17). He was called a fornicator for rejecting God's blessing. He valued his flesh and temporal pleasure (a bowl of soup) over a blessing. He put no value in the long-term blessing of his birthright. Will we trade short-term satisfaction of the flesh (socialism) for our long-term value of our birthright (freedom)? Will we succumb to the lure of free healthcare, universal wages, redistribution of wealth, etc.—a bowl of soup—or will we mix faith with the blessing of freedom? Will we worship government (the bowl of soup) or worship God (the blessing of Abraham)?

The Constitution is my birthright as an American citizen, the Kingdom of God as a Christian. Through faith in Jesus, I have been born again into the Kingdom of God's dear Son. *"Fear not, little flock; for it is your Father's good pleasure to give you the kingdom"* (Luke 12:32). *"He has delivered us from the power of darkness and conveyed us into the kingdom of the Son of His love"* (Col. 1:13). That is my birthright as a citizen of heaven (see Phil. 3:20). I am thankful for both. A bowl of soup is not even tempting.

DARWINISM

Karl Marx and his philosophies on political systems and economics were greatly influenced by Charles Darwin. Darwin's Theory of Evolution declares humans were not created at all, but rather evolved from another life form. He also stated that people are not equal, that some (the elites) are more evolved than others.

Darwin's *Origin of Species* was read and consumed by Karl Marx who believed that the "survival of the fittest" validated his "dialectical conflict." This is where labor and community organizers would create domestic chaos to enable a communist dictator to usurp power.

Darwin was an atheist with a secular worldview that influenced many world leaders who have killed millions of people. Mao Zedong, Vladimir Lenin, Adolf Hitler, Joseph Stalin were all influenced by Darwin's theories. More recently, Margaret Sanger (founder of Planned Parenthood) believed in the superiority of certain races and the need to purge the race of inferior genetics. Her eugenic policies that have taken untold millions of lives through abortion were also influenced by Darwin.

Eugenics is defined as the study of or belief in the possibility of improving the quality of the human species. According to this philosophy, some persons have genetic defects or have inheritable undesirable traits, while others have inheritable desirable traits. Eugenics discourages reproduction by those with so-called negative genetics and encourages reproduction by those who have positive or desirable genetics.

In other words, people considered to have low IQs—"deplorables," weak-minded, disabled, or inferior—need to be sterilized or have some form of birth control. Only the people considered to be highly intelligent, strong-minded, or superior in some way are allowed to have offspring. This is what Darwin's Theory of Evolution has produced. In a culture of darkness, it's acceptable to test expectant mothers for any signs of physical or mental impairments to determine whether a child should live or die. How evil is that? In Darwin's theory of "survival of the fittest," those without

God believe a baby with any physical or mental weakness or handicap should be aborted.

Interestingly, Abraham Lincoln and Charles Darwin were born on the same day, February 12, 1809. Lincoln's view was the polar opposite of Darwin's. Lincoln had a biblical worldview regarding human life, and that view is enshrined in the Constitution. Lincoln stated in his Gettysburg address, November 19, 1863: "Fourscore and seven years ago our fathers brought forth on this continent a new nation, conceived in liberty, and dedicated to the proposition that all men are created equal." That worldview freed the slaves and fulfilled the Scriptures and our highest ideals of our form of government. Darwin's worldview inspired leaders to murder their citizens.

Lincoln still inspires us today to "love our neighbor as ourselves" and "do unto others as you would have done unto you." No slave owner would have supported slavery if he were the slave. Every pro-choice supporter today is thankful for a pro-life mom. If a pro-choice mom suddenly became the actual baby within her own womb, she would quickly become pro-life. Darwin and all his followers and admirers were part of a culture of hate, death, and darkness. Lincoln and his followers were a counterculture loyal to Jesus who has called us to love, life, and light. May our lights shine great in this hour. Lincoln's last act in office was to put the motto "In God We Trust" on our national coins. As a nation, may we turn to God and say, "In God we trust," acting like we really mean it.

Men like him promoted healing of our nation and reconciliation by trusting in God. May we teach our children to love God, their country, and fellow man. May the biblical principles that formed our Constitution once again be the values that reform our great nation. Defending life, liberty, and the pursuit of happiness is a godly thing, not a political one. All politicians swore an oath to uphold these truths. Few today do so, but all should.

There was a generation that understood the dangers of oppressive government as well as the value of freedom. The founders certainly saw it, so they gave us our original documents to resist it and protect us from abusive government. Very few see and understand that today. Those who do are attacked, censored, or canceled. We must speak out and oppose the culture of darkness and tyranny. Our forefathers gave up their fortunes and lives to give us freedom. What are we willing to sacrifice to keep it?

CHAPTER 14

THE WATCHMAN

"But if the watchman sees the sword coming and does not blow the trumpet, and the people are not warned, and the sword comes and takes any person from among them, he is taken away in his iniquity; but his blood I will require at the watchman's hand." So you, son of man: I have made you a watchman for the house of Israel.
—EZEKIEL 33:6-7

In Ezekiel 33:1-11 and Ezekiel 3:17-21 we find the ministry of the watchman. It was the watchman on the wall's responsibility to warn the city of impending danger. "An enemy is coming" was a warning to protect the innocent and unsuspecting. Even now, in military situations, there are people who are stationed at strategic points on bases and in combat whose sole purpose is to be a watchman and warn of incoming danger or invasion.

Whose job is it really to warn a nation of a threat to their families, careers, lives, and even eternity? The media? Politicians? Government? Professors? It is our spiritual leaders' responsibility. We are the watchmen who are to sound the alarm. It would be good and proper for these other institutions to warn of danger. Some in the media do (they are censored). Presidents and politicians of the past have warned of danger on the horizon. Some colleges are teaching truth and the perils of socialism, communism, and Marxism; however, they are few and far between.

Presidents and politicians of the past have warned of danger on the horizon; however, for the most part, modern politics is no longer about policy but rather moral decay and depravity. Government has become less about civil discourse and conduct and more about dismantling of anything noble and decent with our culture. In a dark culture racing toward Marxism, the acquisition of power, corruption, abuse, and personal destruction of anything decent is the order of the day.

So who are the modern-day watchmen? Our spiritual leaders are. They are the watchmen and are tasked with the responsibility of sounding the alarm. As a pastor I have that assignment and that is one of the reasons for writing this book. However, despite this, many leaders refuse to address any cultural or political issues. Corrupt politics is trying to poison every institution of today, including the church. If we think that our silence is going to protect us, then we too are deceived.

The church must guard against becoming political in our pulpits. We cannot allow politics to poison what Paul called the pillar and ground of the truth (see 1 Tim. 3:15). Churches either ignore politics or become political and corrupted by politics. Both are equally dangerous. We cannot have politics in our pulpits, but we must take the pulpits to politics, or we will perish. As watchmen, we better wake up and sound the alarm because the darkness has breached the gates. However, there are pastors afraid of losing members by speaking out on the dangers that are destroying an entire generation's soul. We will lose a lot more than members if we remain silent, not to mention standing before God and giving an account for the lives lost in our silence. Many are afraid of men, and it has become a snare (see Prov. 29:25). We must fear God in this hour and speak up, wake up, and stand up.

Charles Finney, a Presbyterian minister and leader in the Second Great Awakening, warned the clergy of their responsibility to speak God's Word with conviction and boldness to save our nation:

> Brethren, our preaching will bear its legitimate fruits. If immorality prevails in the land, the fault is ours in a great degree. If there is a decay of conscience, the pulpit is responsible for it. If the public press lacks moral discrimination, the pulpit is responsible for it. If the church is degenerate and worldly, the pulpit is responsible for it. If the world loses its interest in religion, the pulpit is responsible for it. If Satan rules in our halls of legislation, the pulpit is responsible for it. If our politics become so corrupt that the very foundations of our

government are ready to fall away, the pulpit is responsible for it. Let us not ignore this fact, my dear brethren; but let us lay it to heart, and be thoroughly awake to our responsibility in respect to the morals of this nation.[1]

Finney was declaring our responsibility as watchmen to speak into all these institutions. They need to be affected by the eternal message of the cross. I wonder how many conferences he would be invited to today.

John Adams, one of the founders and the second U.S. president, said, "Our constitution was made only for a moral and religious people. It is wholly inadequate to the government of any other."[2]

He knew government without moral absolutes, character, and virtue would collapse. He knew people engaged in religious convictions based in pure faith would keep government accountable to serving the people and not let tyranny become the normal state of affairs. He knew that to remove God and His Kingdom principles would give place to evil. James, the brother of Jesus, sums it up well in James 4:7: *"submit to God. Resist the devil and he will flee."* If submitting to God will make Satan flee, then refusing to submit to Him will empower Satan to rule.

In Ezekiel's writings, if the watchman warned people and they disregarded the warning, the consequences of their lack of action fell on them. They were responsible and held accountable. If the watchman failed to warn of the danger coming and the people perished, the watchman was held responsible by God. As leaders in the church, we have a responsibility before God to warn people of danger coming.

Warn them in love of the harm caused by philosophies and systems that are antichrist and destructive to their lives. What could be more harmful than a government system that is atheist (godless)? The only restraint on evil is the church and government founded on Judeo-Christian principles (civil law).

The church is the salt of the earth and light of the world, a city set on a hill (watchman). Government approved by God according to Romans 13:1-5 is to punish evildoers (the guilty) and protect the innocent. We are to pray for all those in authority according to 1 Timothy 2:2: *"that we may lead a quiet and peaceable life in all godliness and reverence."* The apostle Peter said that the role of government in 1 Peter 2:14 was for the *"punishment of evildoers, and for the praise of them that do well."* Governments become corrupt without God, Bible principles, and moral standards according to Scripture. They punish the innocent and protect the guilty, opposing good and celebrating evil.

> Unless the Lord builds the house, they labor in vain who build it; unless the Lord guards the city, the watchman stays awake in vain.
> PSALM 127:1

We are in a partnership with God as watchmen. We need to hear His voice, discern His mind (the mind of Christ), and speak His Word and will. The apostle Paul in Colossians 1 speaks of this great mystery that had been hidden for ages, but now is revealed to God's people, and that mystery was *"Christ in you, the hope of glory"* (Col. 1:27). The following verse says, *"Him we preach,* warning *every man and teaching every man in all wisdom, that we may present every man perfect in Christ Jesus."* Perfect means mature. Our maturity is connected to warnings of danger and teachings of who we are now in Christ.

Paul is preaching our new identity with Christ as well as warning people. Throughout Paul's teaching, there are warnings of false teachers, prophets, wolves in sheep's clothing, and the danger of deception, just to name a few. God's kind of love always warns of things dangerous or damaging to our lives. What kind of love wouldn't warn a child of the dangers of poison, especially when it is disguised as something good? If a bridge is out and innocent people are on the road to destruction, wouldn't it be love to do everything possible to warn and save them?

Many love themselves more than others and won't speak out because of the personal cost in the form of persecution, mockery, and false accusations. When we withhold truth from others for a fear of man, that is self-love, not God's. None of us have a right to withhold truth or reject truth for others. Just because we think someone won't receive truth gives us no right to reject it for them. They have a right to hear it and then reject it for themselves and then be held accountable to God in the day of judgment. The watchman was responsible to share, not decide for the individuals what to do with the information. If we don't warn them and they die in their sins, we are held accountable. Leviticus 19:17-18 reveals how God's kind of love acts, how it cares for others and their wellbeing more than self-preservation:

> *You shall not hate your brother in your heart. You*
> *shall surely rebuke your neighbor, and not bear sin*

because of him. You shall not take vengeance, nor bear any grudge against the children of your people, but you shall love your neighbor as yourself: I am the Lord.

The New Living Translation of verse 17 says to the watchman, "*Confront people directly so you will not be held guilty for their sin.*"

Rebuke here simply is a means of warning like a watchman. Love warns of danger. In a culture of love (God's kind) there is warning of the path we may be on individually or as a nation. Jesus is quoting Leviticus 19:18 in Matthew 22:39 when He says, "You shall love your neighbor as yourself."

We all quote "love our neighbor as ourselves," but many never process the meaning or practicality of how it looks. While love is not condemning of people, it warns of sin's consequences and how rebellion to God's Word will affect them. We are not to be rude or disrespectful but caring enough to speak the truth in love. Satan is known as the "lawless one," and Paul says he comes as an angel of light (see 2 Cor. 11:14). I believe today he comes cloaked in social justice, equity, and fairness. He hijacks God's language and perverts it because he hates humanity and comes to steal, kill, and destroy (see John 10:10). Probably the most deceptive is him proclaiming a false peace that leads to sudden destruction. Paul warns us in 1 Thessalonians 5:1-4:

But concerning the times and the seasons, brethren, you have no need that I should write to you. For you yourselves know perfectly that the day of the Lord so comes as a thief in the night. For when they say,

"Peace and safety!" then sudden destruction comes upon them, as labor pains upon a pregnant woman. And they shall not escape. But you, brethren, are not in darkness, so that this Day should overtake you as a thief.

Notice people will be so blinded by darkness they will be totally unprepared for Jesus' return. They will embrace a false peace and safety that will end in their demise. As children of light, we will be prepared for that day because today we are heeding the warnings associated with darkness.

SPIRITUAL LEADERS

Obey your spiritual leaders and recognize their authority, for they keep watch over your soul without resting since they will have to give an account to God for their work. So it will benefit you when you make their work a pleasure and not a heavy burden.

HEBREWS 13:17 (TPT)

Watch over your souls! Notice we will give an account to God for our work. What work? The work of a watchman. Make no mistake, I understand it takes discipline and diligence to really care about people's lives, especially when you think of all the deadly philosophies that are against Christ and His Kingdom today. They violate every biblical warning and principle of God's Kingdom. These dangerous philosophies have given rise to the glamorization of Marxism.

They allowed Antifa and Black Lives Matter to invade our streets, starting fires, looting, and killing innocent people. Big government, big business, big tech, and big media have all embraced LGBTQA+ behavior by awkwardly and gratuitously injecting it into every aspect of entertainment and education. They lead the way for defunding and dismantling our police, leaving citizens defenseless while crime and murder soars as much as 95 percent in some cities.

Even as I write today there is a huge global campaign underway turning the "vaccinated" against the "unvaccinated" potentially tearing families apart and creating an even deeper divide. The deception even among Christians and Christian leaders is alarming.

In Acts 20:25-31, Paul warns of wolves in sheep's clothing devouring the flock. He fulfills his role in warning them and declares, *"I am innocent of the blood of all men"* (Acts 20:26), and he withheld nothing from them. He shared *"all the counsel of God"* (Acts 20:27). Therefore, as leaders we are to speak out in love.

> *When the righteous are in authority, the people rejoice; but when a wicked man rules, the people groan.*
>
> PROVERBS 29:2

> *Righteousness exalts a nation, but sin is a reproach to any people.*
>
> PROVERBS 14:34

> *Blessed is the nation whose God is the Lord.*
>
> PSALM 33:12

How can a Christian buy into a government system that eliminates God (socialism/communism) or movements that are filled with hate and violence (Marxism)? We cannot fear what man can do to us. We must fear God only.

Fear not, for I am with you; be not dismayed, for I am your God. I will strengthen you, yes, I will help you, I will uphold you with My righteous right hand. Behold, all those who were incensed against you shall be ashamed and disgraced; they shall be as nothing, and those who strive with you shall perish.

ISAIAH 41:10-11

Many are fearful and dismayed with all that is happening in our country. What does it mean to be dismayed? According to *Strong's Concordance* it means "to be nonplussed (looking in amazement or bewildered); to render utterly perplexed; puzzle completely; to depart or turn" (*sha'ah*, H8159).

Dictionary.com defines *dismayed* this way: "to break down the courage of completely, as by sudden danger or trouble; to dishearten thoroughly; to daunt."

Because Marxism, socialism, and communism use every available militant faction to intimidate, threaten, and bully people into submission, many are perplexed, overwhelmed, and afraid to speak up. Anyone standing up today faces threats and assaults on their character, families, and careers. If they are not flat-out afraid, they are most certainly dismayed.

Even spiritual leaders once considered to be fearless are now going AWOL instead of being watchmen on the wall. As I stated earlier, Black Lives Matter, Inc. is a professed Marxist organization. They are trained in Marxist tactics to create hate, division, and chaos. They are a political movement, not a civil rights organization. This is why they attack cops and even black police officers. They won't speak up against black-on-black crime or the disproportionate number of abortions within the black community. It is political, and if you don't sign off on their political agenda "Marxism," then you are a part of the oppressor group. God's counterculture teaches us that black lives really do matter because all lives matter, regardless of skin color. The counterculture is the one who cares about all lives.

The apostle Paul warns us to flee fornication (see 1 Cor. 6:18) and sexual perversion that is like leaven destroying the church (see 1 Cor. 5:6). When we warn people of the dangers of fornication, adultery, incest, homosexuality, etc. we are being a watchman, not hateful or unloving.

The book of Jude admonishes us to *"contend for the faith, warning against immorality, and ungodly men creeping into the church."* John, the apostle of love, warns us of the spirit of antichrist in many passages (see 1 John 2:18,22; 4:3; 2 John 1:7). Many churches have allowed perversions and godless philosophies of men like Karl Marx and organizations such as LGBTQA+ to come into the church, spoiling God's people. These false teachers have caused many of God's people to either compromise their faith or in some cases deny it completely.

The apostle Peter warns of this dangerous path of believers turning from the truth. Second Peter 2:20-22 says:

> *For if, after they have escaped the pollutions of the world through the knowledge of the Lord and Savior Jesus Christ, they are again entangled in them and overcome, the latter end is worse for them than the beginning. For it would have been better for them not to have known the way of righteousness, than*

> *having known it, to turn from the holy command-*
> *ment delivered to them. But it has happened to*
> *them according to the true proverb: "A dog returns*
> *to his own vomit," and, "a sow, having washed, to*
> *her wallowing in the mire."*

Obviously, the path many Christians are on is not a pretty sight. Leaders must warn of the dangers of rejecting truth in this dark hour.

Many of our churches have bought into false narratives that violate God's Word and holiness. Spiritual leaders must warn the innocent and unsuspecting of these dangers. We must also warn the guilty of God's judgment against all ungodliness. These warnings are not mean-spirited or condemning but rather sincere and caring. This is what a counterculture looks like. We must lovingly and peacefully oppose these philosophies and spirit because we care about people.

In Exodus 32:25 Aaron did not protect the people in Moses' absence. Moses saw that Aaron had let the people get completely out of control, much to the amusement of their enemies. His weakness led to moral decline and a free-for-all that ended in disaster. We cannot "go along to get along." There must be loving, peaceful opposition while there is still hope. Aaron should have stood up to the mob who were departing from God's holiness and moral absolutes. We must stand up to the mobs that are enticing God's people to depart from His Word.

Adhering to philosophies that are unscriptural leads to corruption, spoiling God's people with poison to the soul. Truth spoken in love, administered with conviction and passion preserves both society and the church; it also protects both. Many today ignore cultural issues, not only for fear of the world but of fellow Christians. Pastors tend to not make stands on moral issues for fear of losing congregants. If we lose them in spirit and soul, what good is a person in a pew with a lost soul?

If we lose them for righteousness' sake, did we ever have them? Many believe all we need to do is get people saved and not address any cultural issues. While the eternal soul of every person is a priority, God cares about every part of our lives, not just the spiritual. He desires His church to affect culture for good, not for the culture to affect His church for compromise. Yes, we must lead people to Christ, but we are also called to make disciples.

Jeremiah faced a generation that would not hear; still he was faithful to warn them:

> To whom shall I speak and give warning, that they may hear? Indeed their ear is uncircumcised, and they cannot give heed. Behold, the word of the Lord is a reproach to them; they have no delight in it.
>
> JEREMIAH 6:10

Even though people were dull of hearing, he still shared God's Word and warnings of rebelling against truth.

Scriptures use the word *beware of* as a form of warnings of impending danger. Jesus said in Matthew 7:15, "*Beware of false prophets, who come to you in sheep's clothing, but inwardly they are* ravenous wolves." The word *ravenous* means, at its root, "to seize, to catch away, to take by force" (Strong's G727, G726). It also means "extremely hungry," ferocious, greedy, and insatiable. In other words, they have an insatiable hunger rooted in greed to draw you away from Christ for selfish gain. These wolves in our society care for nothing but themselves and have no regard for others, especially future generations.

In Matthew 16:6, Jesus also warns of another threat: *"Take heed and* beware *of the leaven of the Pharisees and Sadducees."* In verse 12 Jesus explains how He is not talking about bread but the doctrine (teaching) of these two groups. *"He did not tell them to beware of the leaven of bread, but of the doctrine of the Pharisees and Sadducees."* In another account, Jesus again warned of the leaven of the Pharisees and then also the leaven of Herod (see Mark 8:15). In Mark 12:38, He tells us to *"beware of the scribes,"* and He goes on to describe their hypocritical behavior.

In Luke 12:1, He tells us to *"beware of the leaven of the Pharisees, which is hypocrisy."* A Christian who falls short of God's righteous living is not a hypocrite. Hypocrites are people pretending to be one person with no intent of being them. It means an "actor." Actors never intend on being the character they pretend to be. They are professional deceivers and get compensated well (fame and fortune). We are to beware of people pretending to be good with no good in their hearts or will to be good. Hidden agendas are the leaven of Pharisees (dead religion) and Herod (corrupt government).

Peter uses the same language in 2 Peter 3:17-18:

> *Beware lest you also fall from your own steadfastness, being led away with the error of the wicked; but grow in the grace and knowledge of our Lord and Savior Jesus Christ.*

Instead of heeding Peter's warning, many are choosing to ignore all the error of the wicked being promoted in our culture.

The counterculture must be faithful to the knowledge of Jesus and His Kingdom principles that lead to freedom, blessings, and prosperity. Filled with passion and compassion, we must lovingly warn the masses of the dangers of Marxism, socialism, and communism. These are all rooted in the spirit of antichrist.

All of us are called to be watchmen at some level. A watchman over our own hearts, our families, our city, and municipal authorities. Being a watchman over the church is an assignment given to all our church leaders. The apostle Peter gives clear instructions to spiritual leaders in 1 Peter 5:1-3:

> *The elders which are among you I exhort, who am also an elder, and a witness of the sufferings of Christ, and also a partaker of the glory that shall be revealed: feed the flock of God which is among you, taking the oversight thereof, not by constraint, but willingly: not for filthy lucre, but of a ready mind, neither as being lords over God's heritage, but being examples to the flock.*

Elders are given oversight, and while they give warnings of danger, they do more than just that. They are to feed and lead the flock with spiritual understanding and knowledge, shaping what they believe and how they behave in God's Kingdom culture. Jeremiah 23:1-4 speaks of God's displeasure with the shepherds. They were called to *"feed My people."*

He goes on to explain the positive results of being fed in verse 4: "*I will set up shepherds over them who will feed them; and they shall* fear no more, *nor be* dismayed, *nor shall they be lacking.*" Wow, being fed by our spiritual leaders produces good fruit in the church. Jeremiah 3:15 states, "*I will give you shepherds according to My heart, who will feed you with knowledge and understanding.*"

Warning of impending danger is important, but teaching people how to walk in Kingdom principles and truth is even more important because it empowers them to avoid danger and prevail in faith. Knowledge and understanding make up wisdom "*the principal thing*" (Prov. 4:7). Without wisdom and understanding God's people will not even be able to discern good and evil.

Lead in Word and Deed

Philippians 3:17-19 declares:

> *Brethren, join in following my example, and note those who so walk, as you have us for a pattern. For many walk, of whom I have told you often, and now tell you even weeping, that they are the enemies of the cross of Christ: whose end is destruction, whose god is their belly, and whose glory is in their shame—who set their mind on earthly things.*

Many today are enemies of the cross and we cannot follow them. Their end is one of darkness and destruction. The things they are glorying in should make them ashamed. We must follow those who set godly examples; those who by example reveal God's justice seated in righteousness and full of mercy; those who, by example, show us how to hear and fear God and to receive His Word; those who, by example, help open our hearts to God's grace, mercy, and truth. Finally, through example, we must follow those who embrace true humility. By doing this, we will eventually move away from a culture of darkness and into God's culture of light achieving favor and blessing in all things. *Amen!*

NOTES

1. Charles Finney, qtd. in "The decay of conscience," https://www.weirtondailytimes.com/opinion/local -columns/2014/08/the-decay-of-conscience.

2. John Adams, "Founders Online: From John Adams to Massachusetts Militia," October 11, 1798, https://founders .archives.gov/documents/Adams/99-02-02-3102.

CHAPTER 15

WHAT DO WE DO NOW?

So you see, faith by itself isn't enough. Unless it produces good deeds, it is dead and useless.
—JAMES 2:17 (NLT)

As the world gets further away from God, what can we do? We must have the kind of faith that leads to actions. James 2:20 confronts us with this challenging truth: "*faith without works is dead.*"

Our first act of faith is to turn to God and, in areas where we are failing, seek Him and His Kingdom (see Matt. 6:33). Where we have lost a biblical worldview and slipped into a secular worldview, we must be willing to change our minds and see things from God's perspective, running at full speed to Him. That all begins with hearing God and obeying out of faith and love. We must ask ourselves the hard questions like: Who have we been listening to? Who really has our ear and attention? Are we allowing the national media to create false narratives? Are we allowing them to consign us to live in fear through their lies and deception? After all, if faith comes by hearing and hearing by the Word of God (see Rom. 10:17), then fear and dismay comes by hearing the six o'clock news, college professors, corrupt politicians, and backslidden preachers.

SEEK HIS KINGDOM FIRST

We must seek God and His Kingdom with the full intent to obey Him rather than man. Loyalty to Jesus and His Word in simple faith obedience is paramount. In Acts 5, Peter and the apostles gave us a perfect example of what it looks like:

> And when they had brought them, they set them before the council. And the high priest asked them saying, "Did we not strictly command you not to teach in this name? And look, you have filled Jerusalem with your doctrine, and intend to bring this Man's blood on us!" But Peter and the other apostles answered and said: "We ought to obey God rather than men."
>
> ACTS 5:27-29

They had been arrested once for disobeying man's law that contradicted God's mandate to go into all the world and preach the gospel in Jesus' name. An angel orchestrated a jailbreak and told them to keep preaching in Jesus' name. Despite being repeatedly forbidden to do so, and under the threat of further persecution and imprisonment, they chose to stay faithful and loyal to Christ, preaching in His name. They understood that their commitment did not end when it clashed with the world. That is true for us as well.

LOVE AND OBEY CHRIST

As a counterculture, we must know what it means to say we love Christ. In John 14:15, Jesus says, *"If you love Me, keep My commandments."* It is out of our love for Jesus that we keep His commandments. Our love is manifest out of our faith obedience to Him as Lord. In John 14:21, Jesus also said, *"He who has My commandments and keeps them, it is he who loves Me."* We should know if we really love God or not. We also should be able to tell who else loves God. His commandments are His Word. *"If you keep My commandments, you will abide in My love, just as I have kept My Father's commandments and abide in His love"* (John 15:10). My favorite of all is Luke 6:46: *"Why do you call me 'Lord, Lord,' and not do the things which I say?"* I love that. Those of us in the counterculture call Him Lord, so we need to obey and simply follow what Jesus has to say.

GOING INTO BATTLE

In 1 Chronicles 12, David is assembling an army for battle. He is drawing from every tribe trained warriors with certain skill sets for battle. To be effective in war, he knew he needed the best from each tribe because they offered different skill sets for battle. In our spiritual warfare in the New Testament, we need different members of the body of Christ to learn from and draw from to war a good warfare. I just want to share from Scripture a few of the skill sets the twelve tribes of Israel had.

From the tribe of Gad these warriors *"were army commanders. The weakest among them could take on a **hundred regular troops**, and the strongest could take on a **thousand!**"* (1 Chron. 12:14 NLT). In verse 24, *"From the tribe of Judah, there were 6,800 warriors armed with **shields and spears**"* (NLT). Then verse 25: *"From the tribe of Simeon, there were 7,100 **brave warriors**"* (NLT). Zebulun offered some things for battle that were interesting and enlightening: *"There were 50,000 skilled warriors...completely **loyal** to David"* (1 Chron. 12:33 NLT).

BE LOYAL TO GOD'S WORD

We must be loyal to Jesus and His Word. It seems people's loyalties are with and to anything but Jesus. We cannot be the watchman God's called us to be without complete loyalty to Jesus as His bride. We must be wed to Him, not the philosophies of today's world or culture. We are to be married to Him, not politics or political parties.

Part of our new identity is our relationship with Jesus where we are one spirit with the Lord (see 1 Cor. 6:17). Just as a husband and wife are one flesh in holy matrimony, we are now united to Jesus and have become His body on the earth. We are to be faithful and loyal to Him as our husband King. Jesus loves us and is a jealous husband, desirous of our total devotion to Him.

First Chronicles 12:32 refers to the sons of Issachar. There were 200 leaders of their tribe who had an interesting skill set: *"All these men understood the signs of the times and knew the best course for Israel to take"* (NLT). We need men and women who are loyal to Jesus and can discern the times and season we are in and communicate what the church needs to do—actions of faith. God is raising up multiple voices from multiple streams with discernment of the times, God's wisdom, and what to do.

Truth has a ring to it, and you can train your ear to hear. Jesus said many times, *"If anyone has ears to hear, let him hear"* (Mark 4:23; 7:16; see also Rev. 2:7,11,17,29; 3:6). As we choose to hear, we become more sensitive to hearing what God is saying. When we choose to not hear, our ability to hear God is impeded.

SPEAK BOLDLY FOR RIGHTEOUSNESS

The counterculture is emerging and making a difference, but we need more men and women who are Christ-centered and heed His voice. Politics is an example of where we see duplicity of loyalty. When politics is lord and we are married to it, Jesus and the Word are compromised for the ascendancy of our political agendas. Jesus and His Word must trump everything (no pun intended).

While I am totally against politics in our pulpits, we must take the pulpit to our politics. From the pulpit, we must stand for life, truth, liberty, and justice for all. We must defend voter rights and election integrity, or our democracy and a representative republic will be gone. Voter ID must be required to ensure legal votes, and we cannot fear being accused of voter suppression and racism. This is the accusation used to silence any opposition to voter fraud and election integrity.

We must eliminate unrestricted mail-in voting, printing of fake ballots, and counting the same ballots multiple times. We must remove any opportunity for hidden algorithms programmed into voting machine software that purposely and automatically alter official vote counts. We must immediately halt illegal votes, out-of-state votes, dead people, and yes, even cartoon characters from voting in our elections (no, really!).

We must also shut the door that allows one individual to cast multiple votes. Finally, web access of our voting systems must be totally eliminated to assure there is no opportunity for foreign or domestic interference. This is just a morsel of the deep corruption contributing to our loss of voter integrity in America and around the world. This must change, or we will be enslaved.

DEMAND INTEGRITY

Anyone who doesn't demand integrity for our elections should not be office. Only those who are corrupt would sanction corruption. Our vote is sacred and our peaceful way of bringing about change. Again, something as simple as voter ID is attacked. You must have an ID to fly on a plane or travel to other countries. (Are all airlines racist?)

An ID is required to drive a car or rent one, enter a bar, purchase liquor or cigarettes, or get a marriage license. Why is it wrong for someone to verify who they are and their age before allowing them to vote? It is not wrong. Every illegal vote cancels out a legal vote. Every dead person's vote undermines the integrity of a live person and the value of their vote.

We must get back to voting on one day and not drag the deadlines along to accommodate fraud. In an absentee ballot, identification must be verified and signed before a notary public. Why would unverified and uncertified mail-in ballots be allowed? Because there are those who want to corrupt the system in order to bring it down. Elected officials must be held accountable to the same laws they impose upon us. These are just a few examples that in a moral and just society would not be controversial.

EXHIBIT PROACTIVE FAITH

The much-needed reforms in our culture can only be achieved by a Third Great Awakening. The hearts of men must be changed first (revival) before the behavior can be changed (reformed). We must lead people to Christ and then make disciples (disciplined followers of Jesus). We must be willing to suffer for our faith, speaking the truth in love—a concept foreign to the average American Christian. We must be willing to lead our nation back to a biblical worldview of government. One that is limited and serves us, not us them. One that is pro-life, pro-liberty, and pro-religious freedom without threat of censorship, persecution, prosecution, or execution for our faith.

Why would we vote for anyone who hates the Constitution and our country? We say we love our children and need to act like it. Get involved in their education and make sure they are not exposed to immorality that defiles their moral innocence before they are mature enough to discern good from evil. Make sure they aren't being taught to hate their country or their fellowman. Get on the school board and protect your children. Get involved in your city council to make sure the police are not defunded knowing they are there to punish evil and protect good (see Rom. 13:1-7; 1 Pet. 2:14).

We must be proactive in our faith and engage in all these cultural issues. For good to prevail, we must be willing to suffer pushback from evil. We must stand for God's Kingdom to come and His will be done in the earth as it is in heaven (see Matt. 6:9). We need to fear God (reverence, be in awe of) and not be afraid of man. *"The fear of man bringeth a snare: but whoso putteth his trust in the Lord shall be safe"* (Prov. 29:25).

Simply put, we must:

- Repent of a secular worldview and adopt a biblical one.

- Seek first the Kingdom of God and His righteousness.

- Obey God versus man, which equals life.

- Be loyal to Jesus over anything else.

- Be a watchman over your heart, family, city, and nation.

- Feed the lambs and sheep with knowledge and understanding, which is wisdom.

- Take the pulpit to politics.

- Stand for life, truth, liberty, and justice for all.

Finally, my dear brothers and sisters:

- Pray and stand for revival (people saved) that leads to reform (make disciples).

- Pray for those in authority.

- Pray for discernment on what is being taught to our children.

- Seek reformation in our schools, police departments, and local government.

- Stand for election integrity and seek to require voter ID for every vote.

- Hold elected officials accountable to the rule of law.

- Vote for people who love this country and desire to follow the Constitution.

- Get involved locally by attending school board meetings and city council meetings to see what is being done and pushed for.

- If led, seek public office to serve your community.

- Do the right thing regardless of the cost.

- Engage by faith and speak the truth in love.

These are just a few of the many things we can do to stand for truth, liberty, and justice. As we seek God and His Kingdom first, He is faithful to lead and guide us into all truth and show us what we can do to labor with Christ in setting our feet back on a righteous path. "Critical Grace Theory" is the hope and healing of the nations. Get dressed and stay clothed in God's armor. It is time to be awakened and make a stand! As the counterculture it is time to bring heaven to earth and make a difference for the praise of His glory.

CONCLUSION

Not everyone is called to speak out publicly against evil, though every Christian is called to resist evil and fight the good fight of faith in making a stand for truth and righteousness. As Bible believers, we must be prepared for false accusations and verbal assassinations of our character and integrity.

Revelation 12:11 speaks of us overcoming by the *"blood of the Lamb and by the word of their testimony, and they did not love their lives to the death."* This book of the Bible often speaks of the death of the saints by the spirit of antichrist. We may not have to give our lives today for righteousness, holiness, purity, godliness, and faithfulness to the words of Jesus, but we will be persecuted at some level for righteousness' sake (see 2 Tim. 3:12).

To many this may sound radical, maybe somewhat like a talk show host with their hair on fire, or a GOP fanatic who seems defensive. But what if?

What if this was like Noah who spent years telling the people of imminent destruction if they did not repent (see Heb. 11:7; 2 Pet. 2:5)? Jeremiah, the prophet, was faithful in declaring impending judgment and captivity because of the peoples' sins and silence. How about the prophet Hosea who called out Israel for their fornication and playing the role of a prostitute? Was Jonah radical when he was spit up on the beach of Nineveh and called that nation to repentance for their wickedness? Many other prophets, called by God to speak to His people, were mocked, shamed, persecuted, sometimes even prosecuted, and killed.

What if this sounds like the apostle Paul warning people of false prophets and teachers that would try and deceive God's people—some he even specifically named publicly (see 2 Tim. 4:14)? Last, but certainly not least, what if this sounds like Jesus who warned the hypocrites of the coming judgment for their duplicity in actions, calling them snakes, vipers, whitewashed tombstones, full of dead men's bones (see Matt. 3:7; 12:34; 23:27). Or what about when He overturned the tables of the moneychangers in the temple declaring that they had made the house of prayer into a den of thieves (see Matt. 21:12-13)? Wow! I wonder if His voice inflection or resonance would have met the new standards of "being nice" or "woke" or "politically correct."

I understand why the prophets were stoned and killed—because of their steadfast obedience to speak the Word of the Lord.

I aspire to be innocent of the accusations thrown my way but to be found guilty of hearing and obeying God. If taken to court and charged with being a Christian, may enough evidence be found to convict. May all of us as Bible-believing, truth-wielding, faith-standing, Holy Spirit-praying, armor-bearing warriors be found faithful and loyal to Jesus and the Kingdom of God.

God bless!

ABOUT DUANE SHERIFF

Duane Sheriff is the Founding Pastor and Senior Elder of Victory Life Church, a multi-campus church which is headquartered in Durant, OK. Pastor Duane travels the world speaking at conferences, churches, and he is also a frequent teacher at Charis Bible College. He has a passion to help people grow in Christ and to see people discover their purpose. His first book, *Identity Theft,* was released in 2017 and since then has authored two more books: *Our Union with Christ* and *Better Together.* Pastor Duane and his wife, Sue, have four children and eleven grandchildren.

For free teachings by Pastor Duane visit his website at
www.pastorduane.com

OUR VISION

Proclaiming the truth and the power of the Gospel of Jesus Christ with excellence. Challenging Christians to live victoriously, grow spiritually, know God intimately.

Connect with us on

f Facebook @ **HarrisonHousePublishers**

and 📷 Instagram @ **HarrisonHousePublishing**

so you can stay up to date with news about our books and our authors.

Visit us at **www.harrisonhouse.com**

for a complete product listing as well as monthly specials for wholesale distribution.